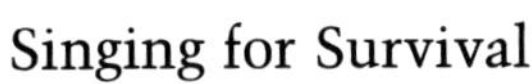

Singing for Survival

Singing for Survival

Songs of the Lodz Ghetto, 1940–45

GILA FLAM

UNIVERSITY OF ILLINOIS PRESS
Urbana and Chicago

Publication of this book was made possible in part by a grant from the
Lucius N. Littauer Foundation.

Manufactured in the United States of America
C 5 4 3 2 1

This book is printed on acid-free paper.

Library of Congress Cataloging-in-Publication Data

Flam, Gila, 1956–
Singing for survival : songs of the Lodz ghetto, 1940–45 / Gila Flam.
p. cm.
Includes bibliographical references and index.
ISBN 0-252-01817-6 (alk. paper)
1. Jews—Poland—Łódź—Music—History and criticism. 2. Jews—Poland—Łódź—Persecutions. 3. Holocaust, Jewish (1939–1945)—Poland—Łódź. 4. Songs—Poland—Łódź—20th century—History and criticism. 5. Jews—Poland—Łódź—Music. 6. Songs—Poland—Łódź—20th century. I. Title.
ML3776.F62 1992
782.42162'92404384—dc20 90-27846
CIP
MN

The song was the only truth.

Miriam Harel,
Holocaust survivor

Contents

Preface

This is the story of a community created and destroyed by the Nazis. The people of this community, the Lodz ghetto, had neither a free social organization nor a geographical or politically independent role, yet they created their own music culture shaped by their specific needs and the practices possible in their situation.

The Lodz ghetto became a community different from the one that existed before World War II. However, this community continued to exist in the minds and memories of its survivors after the war. The war made the community a communitas—a group of people who shared particular experiences and memories. The music culture, with its multifarious parts, depended on that community and its search for a source of unity in times of tragedy and remembrance.

The music culture of the Lodz ghetto is in some ways unique, yet it provides a concentrated look at Eastern European Jewish music culture in general. This culture points to the differences that existed between music as street entertainment and the individual songs created within a tightly constricted musical context at home. It distinguishes group singing among youth sharing a common ideology, group singing of workers forced to become a group, and reminiscences of the prewar professional popular culture of the Yiddish theater. Although these contexts for singing existed before the war, both the content and the meaning of the songs changed in response to the events of the time.

To this music culture another facet was added after the war—commemoration. In the interviews I have conducted, the survivors reconstructed the songs sung in the ghetto and their contexts, but they did not wish to see the ghetto songs performed in commemoration ceremonies that they organized in Israel. Why did the survivors choose not to recall these original ghetto songs? Why did they not create new songs for the new context? These and other questions will be addressed and answered in this study.

I hope that the reader will follow my journey through the life histories of the Lodz ghetto survivors interwoven with their songs. The songs of the Lodz ghetto as presented in this book embody the history of this community, the lives of its inhabitants, and the unifying forces that drew them together.

Singing for Survival is an attempt to understand the role of singing in times of duress. Though it focuses on a particular community during the Holocaust, it has a universal message for each and every one of us to remember.

A Note on Transliteration and Translation

The translations from Yiddish and Hebrew in this book are mine. The translations from Polish are by my parents, Esther and Shlomo Flam, who have kindly spent time in helping me to understand Polish words in this specific context.

Yiddish orthography follows the standard YIVO system (Weinreich 1968). The Yiddish transcriptions are not standardized since the standard Yiddish romanization follows the principally Lithuanian pronunciation, which was not spoken by the subjects of this book. The Yiddish song texts, therefore, will be left in the personal speech pattern of the singer.

Transcriptions from Hebrew follow *The American National Standard Manual for Romanization* (1975) except in cases of names and terms that already have familiar English forms (e.g., "Miriam" rather than the phonetic "Miryam").

Polish and German names will appear in their English form when these exist. Other non-English terms are italicized.

Since people's voices are the core of this book, I have not made the testimonies more literary than they were, nor have I rendered them into smooth, idiomatic English.

Acknowledgments

In gratitude I acknowledge the cooperation of the survivors of the Lodz ghetto whose goodwill and devotion made this study possible. I am grateful to have known these people; they shared with me their past painful experience and their continuing belief in life and humanity.

I would like to thank Esther Abramovitz, Arieh Ben-Menaḥem, Miriam Harel, Leah Hochberg, Rivkah Pinḥasik, Yaakov Rotenberg, Arieh Shaar, Itka Slodowsky, Yeḥiel Tal-Shir, Arieh Tal-Shir, Yeḥiel Frenkiel, and Michael Tenenbaum, survivors of the Lodz ghetto whom I met in Israel; and Yaakov Bressler, Freda Burns, Lucille Eichengreen, Yaakov Flam, Esther Milch, Pinchas Shaar, and Abraham Weberman, who reside in America. All of my informants shared songs and stories on condition that no use, reuse, or commercial use would be made of the material except with my permission. I owe my new knowledge to these teachers, who know as I do now the importance of the lesson of remembering to prevent the repetition of crimes against humanity.

I am grateful to the institutions who supported me both financially and spiritually by acknowledging the importance of my work. I feel special gratitude to The 1939 Club for sponsoring my work through their fellowship; to the PEO Sisterhood for awarding me the Peace International Scholarship and for their considerations beyond the financial support offered over a period of three years; and to the Memorial Fund for Jewish Art in the Diaspora which supported my work from Jerusalem.

I would also like to express my thanks to Michael Nutkiewicz, the director of the Martyrs Memorial and Museum of the Holocaust in Los Angeles, for asking me to lecture in that institution, thus enabling me to meet some of the Lodz survivors who enriched my knowledge; to Cantor Samuel Kelemer of Temple Beth-Am in Los

Angeles (where I served as a music teacher) for sharing with me his knowledge and introducing me to unpublished material; and to Flo Kinstler, who shared with me her approach in studying Holocaust survivors.

To my former teachers at the University of California Los Angeles and other institutions I owe a debt of gratitude for their advice and intellectual guidance. I owe special thanks to Prof. Janet Hadda and Prof. James Porter for their deep understanding and support.

To my friends I extend my gratitude for their technical and emotional assistance. Special thanks to Bret Werb, who read every word of this manuscript. Without his advice and care this work would not have been possible.

While writing this book I shared my thoughts and ideas with my colleagues at the United States Holocaust Memorial Museum in Washington, D.C., to whom I would like to express my gratitude. Many thanks to Dr. Michael Berenbaum, Martin Smith, and Jeshajahu Weinberg for their support and inspiration, and to Scott Miller for his practical comments and daily support.

Many thanks also to my colleagues at the YIVO Institute (Yidisher Visnshaftlekher Institut) for Jewish Research for their valuable comments about my manuscript. Eleanor Gordon Mlotek made useful comments on the origins of the songs, and Marek Web read a draft of this book with a critical though constructive eye. I would also like to extend my thanks to the YIVO Archives, which granted me permission to include some of the photographs from the Zonabend Collection. Special thanks to Roberta Newman for her help and patience in searching for these photographs and making them available to me.

I would like to extend my appreciation to the World Congress for Jewish Culture (CYCO) and the Educational Department of the Workmen's Circle in New York for permitting me to include in this book three of the songs composed by David Beyglman and Isaiah Shpigl. Special thanks to Joseph Mlotek for his help in this matter.

Very special thanks to Philip Bohlman for reading this manuscript with care and to Mark Slobin for his general comments which brought this book to its present stage. To Judith McCulloh, executive editor at the University of Illinois Press, I would like to express special thanks for her faith, patience, and advice.

I thank my wonderful parents, Esther and Shlomo Flam, for their lifetime support. Special gratitude goes to my father, who gave me his personal photographs as well as photographs he discovered in the Lodz ghetto after his liberation (on 19 January 1945), and who granted me permission to include some of them in this book. I would also like to thank my father for his comments on this book as well as for his assistance in locating and interviewing many of his past and present friends from the Lodz ghetto. To both my mother and my father I can not find better words than to say *Todah Rabah.*

Introduction

I was led to undertake a study of Yiddish song by my love of music and the Yiddish language. But I soon found myself drawn to one particular aspect of the repertoire—an especially imperiled one.

The ghetto songs of World War II touched my emotions in a very personal way. Both my parents survived the war in Poland and they shared with me vivid recollections of their experiences. Interviews with other ghetto survivors convinced me of the importance of the repertoire and also of the urgent need to record and preserve these songs before it was too late.

As an ethnomusicologist, I was versed in various philosophies and methodologies enabling me to deal with the variety of world music from a consistent perspective. My involvement with the ghetto repertoire, I found, personalized and refined my academic training, bringing home the subjectivity at the core of all the arts—and humanities.

If any single personality was responsible for setting the tone of my research and subsequent work, it was a ghetto survivor I encountered in Israel. A woman just then approaching sixty, Miriam Harel was a poet, writer, and singer who astonished me with her songs and commentary. I began to understand that I was confronting music as an avenue for the human spirit, of human expression amid inhuman conditions. Miriam Harel's ability to express herself—and the depth of her expression—further convinced me of the need to pursue this investigation.

As I saw it, part of my task was to determine the meaning of the songs in terms of the aesthetic and symbolic values attributed to them by my subjects. As Miriam put it: "The song was the only truth. The Nazis could take everything away from us, but they could not take singing from us. This remained our only human expression."[1]

The song was the only truth for Miriam Harel and many survivors. But can the same be said for all people? And does this truth apply to an "outsider" like me? Such were my thoughts while shaping the material for this book. The songs seemed to me to be the conduit of truth rather than the truth itself. But on deeper reflection, the idea of song as something that stands apart from reality is an essential theme of my work. The song as an autonomous entity, as an expression of freedom, offered me an insight into my personal history I could never have obtained otherwise.

I have chosen to tell the story of one ghetto, the Lodz ghetto, where my father was interned during the war. The cultural life of this particular ghetto has been very little researched until recently, a fact that encouraged me to carry out this project.

To collect the songs of the Lodz ghetto, I sought out and interviewed survivors, locating them in Israel and the United States (Los Angeles, Detroit, and New York).

My interviews were all conducted in the homes of the individual subjects, mainly in Hebrew, Yiddish, and English. Some of the survivors were explicit and could express themselves verbally, while others could not find the right words to describe their experiences. All of them went through the process of selective memory long after the event, and as a result were able to recall certain things only fragmentarily. Most of these survivors were young people between the ages of eleven and twenty during the war. Their wartime experiences were perceived through youthful eyes, their lives before the war through the eyes of children. Forty years later they told their life histories from the perspective of mature adults.[2]

In the main, these people came from traditional Jewish families, though primarily not from Orthodox or Hassidic backgrounds. Clearly, the small community I describe, a cross section of Polish Jewry, cannot represent a complete portrait of the Lodz ghetto. The lack of information on cultural life of the Jews in Lodz before the war does not allow me to portray accurately the fullness of Jewish life and thus show the change in their life and community. The Holocaust brought to an end the sources as well as the full historical perspective needed to look at that period.

My description of life and the community before the time of the ghetto is based on scattered information drawn from the survivors' life histories and some speculations I've made based on American Jewish cultural life in the interwar period. I have focused on the informants' lives in the ghetto, giving a brief summary of their experiences before and after this period of their lives. My first questions to them were always directed to the cultural life of the ghetto and the role of music in it.

Nowadays, the survivors of the Lodz ghetto do not form a community in the common sense of the word, that is to say, they do not form a group of individuals who share and interact in a particular geographical area. However, they are a "communitas" in the same sense described by Victor Turner (1969), a group of people who share particular experiences and memories, and as such they redefine themselves as *landsmen*—people from the same hometown (or in this case, people interned in the same place), who meet once or twice a year in a memorial observance or a "commemoration ceremony."[3]

To the informants I was an outsider, fortunate enough not to have endured their sufferings. However, my familiarity and sympathy with their historical and emotional experiences drew me close to them, and I was often received with warmth, openness, and cooperation.

In more than one hundred hours of interviews conducted during 1983–86, I recorded the life stories and songs of twenty-one survivors of the Lodz ghetto. From these twenty-one I selected five exemplary subjects whose stories were more coherent, contained more information, and, on a personal level, moved me more emotionally than the others.

The songs I collected were transcribed and their texts translated from Yiddish and Polish into English; I then classified them according to original context of singing: street songs, domestic songs, theater songs, youth organization songs, workplace songs, and contemporary Holocaust commemoration songs.

My use of the term "Holocaust song" builds on the usage by earlier scholars, particularly Kaczerginsky and Rubin, but is somewhat broader in scope. Shmerke Kaczerginsky (1908–54), who published the first anthology of Holocaust songs, titled his collection *Lider fun di getos un lagern* (Songs of the ghettos and camps) (1948). A ghetto survivor who was also a singer, writer, poet, and song collector, Kaczerginsky typifies the "insider" type of observer—one who was on the scene, writing of his own time, place, and people.

Ruth Rubin (1907–), a contemporary of Kaczerginsky, writing from a North American context, of necessity approaches the songs from a "removed" perspective. In her extensive study of the Yiddish folksong (1979) she attempts to categorize the Holocaust repertoire. As with the rest of her work, the song types she supplies are derived from the textual themes (i.e., the plight of the children, resistance, hope).

The present book, like that of Kaczerginsky, though forty years after the fact, is based on survivors' accounts. Like Rubin, I have been forced to adopt a "decontextualized" (or "modified contextual") perspective. Nevertheless, I have attempted to group the material into meaningful categories based on the settings in which they were sung.

As this book will tell, the singers availed themselves of a varied and eclectic repertoire during their period of internment. When confronted with the question "What did you sing in the ghetto?" they recalled songs learned in early youth, prewar popular ditties, Zionist patriotic hymns, and the like. In other words, a large number of songs do not correspond to the common definition of this repertoire. A similar dichotomy arises in relation to the repertoire of later Holocaust commemoration ceremonies, which includes numerous pieces stemming from sources much earlier—and also later—than the Holocaust period itself.

My own definition of "Holocaust song" takes into account both content and context. Thus I use the term primarily in its commonly understood sense to refer to a song composed in the ghettos or camps of World War II whose lyric content relates to this particular historical period. The second definition is supplied by the songs' context, and expands the temporal, spatial, and personal frames of the ghetto songs to include material not previously considered.

My definition deviates from those of other scholars of Jewish music. For many of these scholars, lyrics are the likeliest avenue of approach to delineation of song types. Thus Binder (1952, ed. Heskes 1971), Kipnis (1949), Cahan (1952, 1957), Beregovski (1938 and 1962, both ed. Slobin 1982), Rubin (1979), Idelsohn (1929), and Slobin (1976 and 1982) set down basic categories of Yiddish folksong such as cradle songs, education, play songs, love songs, marriage songs, Sabbath songs, and holiday songs. These categories would have been useless for the Lodz ghetto song repertoire and would have forced me to describe what the repertoire excludes instead of what it includes. Kaczerginsky (1948) felt the need to invent new categories for the songs of the ghettos and camps, but his categories are ambiguous: 1. Never Say; 2. Ghetto Life; 3. Treblinka; 4. Counteract. All these categories are named after the first song in each group, and the differences among the four are unclear to me.

After collecting the songs of the Lodz ghetto, I felt the need to devise my own categories which should not be exclusively concerned with the text. The other option was to categorize the songs according to musical categories, such as dance tunes or marching tunes, but this again would not allow me to categorize the songs in a significant way. The songs of the Lodz ghetto are unique in their content. Their musical language is derived mainly from existing prewar melodies or composed in the popular style of the Yiddish theater of Yiddish folk singing. Indeed, these songs are rewriting the history of the Jewish community and require a new approach to uncover their meaning. Thus, I came to classify them according to their performance—the context of singing.

The book will unfold the story of the Lodz ghetto in song. The songs are not only words set into musical tones, each song in its context is, in fact, a motive and motivation for survival, a complex of symbols and activities for a community purposefully restrained from pursuing a traditionally meaningful life. The songs comment and testify on the ongoing events and at the same time provide an aesthetic experience or diversion from reality. These dichotomies will be described in the book as they embody the history of the community up to the present.

The songs are classified, presented, and interpreted according to their context in light of the historical background (chapter 1) and along with the life histories of the singers. Thus chapters 2 and 3 are devoted to street songs; chapter 4 is devoted to domestic songs, chapter 5 to theater songs, youth organization songs, and workplace songs; and chapter 6 focuses on the contemporary songs sung in commemoration ceremonies of the communitas.

Most of these songs are part of Yiddish (and universal) popular music. In style and origin they are similar to popular songs in America, "written for, and most often performed by, a single voice or a small group of singers, accompanied by either a single chord-playing instrument or some sort of band, ensemble, or small orchestra; usually first performed and popularized in some form of secular stage entertainment, and afterward consumed (performed or listened to) in the home" (Whitcomb 1973 : 1).

The Yiddish song in the ghetto continued to be part of this repertoire derived from Polish, American, and Yiddish popular music. However, it had its own source of inspiration from the Yiddish folksong tradition and Jewish religious music, especially the cantorial tradition of Eastern Europe.

Although Yiddish popular music was dominant among Jews in the cities of Poland and America (as elsewhere) at the beginning of the twentieth century, it received, until recent times, scant attention from scholars. Until Slobin's groundbreaking studies of American popular music (1982), even the American repertoire remained untouched, and the Eastern European repertoire was completely neglected (except for when it had some relevance to its American offspring).

The central factor that may account for the scholarly neglect of this rich repertoire is a lack of historical perspective, coupled with a bias by musicologists or music scholars toward liturgical music. Thus, as mentioned, the events of the war years, coupled with the worldwide decline of Yiddish, brought this popular music to an end before scholars could gain perspective. One scholar has noted, "A popular art form requires a home community (be it ever so humble) to nurture and respond to it, and above all popular songwriters are loath to write in a language few can understand. Certain items in the Yiddish pop repertoire, . . . remain evergreen, and some have passed into the pop mainstream or into folklore. However, the genre's momentum was throttled, needless to say, by the events of the war years, and the song style could not have survived the discontinuity of tradition undiminished" (Werb 1987 : 11).

Thus this book opens a window to a lost repertoire of the Yiddish popular song. It presents and interprets the songs in the light of the historical context (the text) and the musical context (the melodies). As described by Hamm, popular songs "were inner and outer reality made into luscious slices of words and music: popular song—more powerful than all your bombs. . . . Admittedly dancing was the absolute base of all pop music (and, indeed, all music) but running a close second was singing" (Hamm 1979 : 127). In the ghetto, singing was first, as dancing was a rare occurrence.

The role of singing is the heart of this work. As a corollary, however, I will explore the diversity of song within the Lodz ghetto (which after all, was not a homogeneous society). From the survivors' accounts, and through an analysis of their repertoire, this work will attempt to answer the question What was the meaning of song and singing in the Lodz ghetto?

NOTES

1. Interview, Kiryat Bialik, 6 August 1983.

2. Florabel Kinstler, in her dissertation concerned with the psychological effects of survivors' testimonies, distinguishes between two groups of survivors: "adult survivors," people who were adolescents or young adults during the Holocaust, those sixteen and over at the war's end (or fifty-seven and over at the time of her interviewing them), and "child survivors," those under sixteen at the war's end (or under fifty-seven when interviewed). Ac-

cording to these categories, most of my informants are adult survivors. For the results of her study see Kinstler (1986).

3. A "commemoration ceremony" is a yearly memorial observance based on the Jewish ritual *yortsayt*. Only in this instance whole communities, rather than individuals, are memorialized; see the discussion in chapter 6. I recorded all interviews and commemoration ceremonies on cassette tapes; they are part of my private collection.

For more about the notion of community and its folk music, see Bohlman (1988), chapter 4. Information about the notion of communitas and its experience can be found in Turner (1969), esp. 78–104.

1

The Historical Context

Lodz: The Ghetto

This is how Miriam Harel described the first day of the war, 1 September 1939:

> I was not even fifteen years old when the Nazis came into power. We lived in the well-to-do district of Lodz. . . . I was just to begin my ninth year of school. There were no clouds in the sky, so far as I was concerned. Then, on the first of September, 1939, suddenly—yes, suddenly—I saw people gathering in the streets, discussing the news they have heard on the radio. Everyone could hear the loud barking. This was Hitler's voice. Hitler told the world why the German people must fight for their rights and make the Third Reich the greatest nation in the whole world. He also said that the greatest criminals in the world are the Jews. He would take care of the Jewish question. Many people cried. We children were excited but not troubled. Generally speaking, nobody knew what was going to happen. I do not mean at the war front, but what was going to happen to us, the Jews. After four days they came to our town. Immediately the killing began. They grabbed the rich, our professionals, intellectuals, and religious leaders. Nobody would ever see them again. Everyone in the streets was in great danger. We were ordered to put a sign on our sleeves to identify our Jewishness, and death was the punishment for disobedience. The tragic September went by, but each new day brought a new series of disasters. The robberies, murders, kidnappings, and killings had only just begun.[1]

On 17 September, the Soviet army in collusion with Hitler invaded Poland from the east. The Poles surrendered, and on 28 September the U.S.S.R. and Nazi Germany partitioned Poland: western and central Poland, with a population of some twenty-two million, came under German rule. Wartheland (*Warthegau*), with the Polish industrial city of Lodz (having the second largest Jewish population in Poland), was incorporated into Hitler's expanding empire by a decree he issued on 8 October 1939.

About a month later, on 7 November 1939, Lodz was practically incorporated into the Reich and was subject to intensive germanization. Its name changed officially to Litzmannstadt to glorify General Karl Litzmann, who was killed near Lodz in World War I. German was proclaimed the official language (all street names were changed; for example, Lutomierska Street became Hamburgerstrasse), and the use of Polish by Jews was prohibited for most occasions.

Lodz, the leading textile-manufacturing center of Eastern Europe and the industrial heart of Poland, was now to serve the Third Reich as the center of industry in the eastern provinces. As Solomon F. Bloom describes the city's imperiled situation during these events:

> Lodz fell without a blow barely a week after the war broke out in September 1939. It was bound to be a city of special interest to Germany. With its twelve hundred enterprises and two million spindles, it had long been famous as the Manchester of the east. In a century, it had grown from a village to a city of nearly three quarters of a million people, next to Warsaw the largest in the country. Here the Germans and the Jews repeated their traditional common role in Eastern Europe: they rather than the Poles had developed Lodz. (1966:31)

As Miriam Harel described it, the Nazi authorities used constant terror to forestall any possible resistance. Anti-Jewish ordinances were instituted toward the end of 1939: prohibition of religious ceremonies and prayers in synagogues during the High Holidays, freezing of bank accounts, forced labor, disbanding of prewar Jewish organizations and institutions, curfew between 7:00 P.M. and 8:00 A.M., display of the mark *Jude* in yellow letters in front of every Jewish shop, confiscating of wireless radios, a prohibition on the possession of wagons, pushcarts, and similar forms of private transportation, wearing the Star of David, a ban against Jewish use of municipal public transportation, and more.

Shortly thereafter came the notion of resettling the Jews in a closed small section of the city—the ghetto. The Nazi propaganda claimed that the ghettos were necessary in order to protect the non-Jews from the Jews, as Jews were said to be carriers of epidemic illnesses. In many instances the Jews were also accused of cooperating with Germany's enemies; this was the reason they had to be shut up in ghettos. Preparations had begun early in the winter of 1939 and led to an order to close the ghetto issued on 30 April by the chief of police in Lodz, S.S.-Brigadenführer Johannes Schaeffer. On 1 May the ghetto was sealed off from the outside world.

The use of the term "ghetto" was misleading, because Jewish ghettos originated in Rome and Alexandria as a means of self-defense against possible persecutions. Later, in medieval times in Europe, the church advocated the ghetto as a means of separating Christians from Jews, transforming the voluntary Jewish quarter into an obligatory ghetto, walled and guarded. Jews had to carry identifying badges, though they could leave the ghetto to conduct their business outside. The Gentiles could enter the ghetto to conduct business as well. It was not a prison. In Lodz, as in other Nazi ghettos, the Jews were not allowed to leave the ghetto area, and entry into the ghetto by Germans or Poles was forbidden.

The first experiment with establishing a ghetto in Poland was in Piotrkow on 28 October 1939, though the plan was abandoned. Lodz, then, became the first city in which plans became fact, and Jews were enclosed in a wire-fenced section of the city. The ghetto was established in the Bałuty quarter, the most neglected northern district of the city, and in Stare Miasto (the Old Town), known for its poverty and underworld characters. Along with suburban areas of Marysin, the ghetto initially measured 4.3 square kilometers, and was reduced in February 1941 to 3.8 square kilometers. Within the ghetto, housing conditions were critical. Most of the apartments contained one room with no running water or electricity. The average occupancy per room was 3.5 persons. Most of the ghetto inhabitants lost all their property when they left their city homes, and the rest was confiscated gradually.

The creation of the Lodz ghetto was viewed by the occupiers as a temporary solution, for they intended to deport all Jews from the newly annexed Polish territories. Despite its provisional character, however, the ghetto was to last, if not in its entirety, until the summer of 1944. At this time it was the only ghetto left in Polish territory.

By general agreement, the number of Jews in Lodz fluctuated between 230,000 and 250,000 (there are no authoritative sources). In addition, 5,000 Gypsies from Austria were deported to the Lodz ghetto between the fifth and ninth of November 1941. A Gypsy camp area in the ghetto was designated and separated from the Jewish population of the ghetto.

The Lodz ghetto gradually became a large slave labor camp of workshops and factories. Hunger, overcrowding, and lack of sanitation caused epidemics, mainly typhus. The number of deaths increased daily, as could be seen from the reports of *The Chronicle of the Lodz Ghetto 1941–1944* (Dobroszycki 1984).

The ghetto administration was concentrated in two branches of German local authority: the political and police forces, and the administrative and economic division. The former included the local police (Ger.: *Schutzpolizei, Schupo* for short), the criminal police (Ger.: *Kriminalpolizei, Kripo* for short), and the secret state police (Ger.: *Geheime Staatspolizei, Gestapo*). The latter was chiefly concentrated in the municipality of Lodz.

The city municipality, as opposed to the political and police branch, was supposed to fulfill functions that the occupier defined as constructive and whose aim was to put all the ghetto's labor force to work. To that end, a department with broad authority was created first as the Department of Food Supply and Economics, and later, from October 1940, as the Ghetto Administration (*Gettoverwaltung*). Among the *Gettoverwaltung*'s specific tasks was to receive orders from interested parties of the Reich's war industry and from private companies, and to supply the ghetto with raw materials and machines. At the same time, the *Gettoverwaltung* supervised the ghetto's entire range of internal affairs, which was handed to the Jewish Council. The head of the *Gettoverwaltung* in Lodz throughout the war was Hans Biebow.

Within the ghetto, there was the internal Jewish administration which was created by an order of the German authorities. The Jewish Council arose earlier than the ghetto and was responsible for transporting the Jewish population from all districts of Lodz to the ghetto, to find housing for them, and later to provide some form of social existence. The more important departments of the internal administration were the Jewish police, the fire department, the department of economics, and the department of social welfare.

Within the Jewish administration, the dominant figure was Mordechai Chaim Rumkowski, who was appointed by the Germans on 13 October 1939 as their official Jewish ruler of the ghetto, and called the Eldest of the Jews. In Lodz, the head of the Council of Elders, the *Altestenrat,* or more accurately, *Beirat* (known in other ghettos as *Judenrat*), existed only as an advisory group since the power was quickly seized by the chairman of the council, Rumkowski.

One should remember that contact with the outside world was in German hands as was the control of food, which was at that time handled by the Department of Food Supply and Economics, headed by Hans Biebow. The isolation was compounded by the removal of telephones from private homes and the confiscation of radios. Mail was undependable and censored. As described by the historian Lucy Dawidowicz, "Warsaw and Lodz, with the largest Jewish populations, were the most tightly, almost hermetically, sealed ghettos" (1975:205–6).

Yehuda Bauer accords with Dawidowicz and describes the situation in more detail:

> Lodz was the most completely isolated ghetto—there was literally no possibility of any contact with the outside world. The ghetto was fenced with barbed wire and exits were guarded by police who had standing orders to shoot to kill. Entry by non-Jews was also well-nigh impossible. Food was therefore limited to that supplied by the supervisors of the ghetto, whereas in other ghettos smuggling and economic exchange eased the situation to a smaller or greater degree. The poverty was such, however, that the starved population could not buy even meager supplies provided. (1982 : 154)

The ghetto's first year was relatively calm, so much so that it might have appeared that the Germans had achieved their aim and would draw the line there. The Jews had been settled in a closed quarter of the city, where it was easier to supervise them and use them as a slave labor force concentrated in various workshops. Raw material and some food were sent into the ghetto, while the products of the ghetto were then brought out for German use. The prices of food, however, were much higher than the prices of the products, and predictably, hunger and starvation increased.

A system of food rationing (except for bread) was introduced in the ghetto on 2 June 1940, and thereafter ration cards regulated life in the ghetto. In 1940 the populace tried to resist. Hunger demonstrations and similar disturbances broke the calm during the first year of the ghetto. All were suppressed by the Jewish police (Ger.: *Ordnungsdienst*) and the German police.

The entire Jewish quarter was cut off from the network of municipal services, including electricity, fire protection, and mail. The Germans handed over to Rumkowski the ghetto's administration in its entirety including peace-keeping, economic, and social affairs. They endowed him with broad powers as the basis for the ghetto's so-called internal autonomy.

Living conditions deteriorated in the ghetto's second year. Communal, cultural, and social institutions were active until the end of 1941. The school system operated, child care was provided by a network of children's homes, orphanages, summer camps, and free meal programs. Important social programs for ghetto youth such as the *hakhsharah* (youth training camp) and *kibbutz* (youth agricultural settlement) operated in Marysin. Theater performances and literary and musical events were conducted in the Culture House until 1942.

On 7 December 1941, the first Nazi death camp, in Chelmno, began its experimental run.[2] The first to be gassed in the killing vans were Jews from several towns near Lodz, the entire Gypsy camp from Lodz, and the Jews of Lodz. Between 7 and 14 December 1942, 6,400 people were killed in Chelmno. Between January and May 1942, 54,990 persons were killed—more than one third of the ghetto population. From 16 January 1942 to April 1943, the ghetto was obliged to deliver 1,000 people daily, an order carried out by the ghetto administration according to a variety of criteria described below.[3]

During the ghetto's second year, the Germans began resettling Jews from Western Europe into the ghetto. Almost twenty thousand Jews from Bohemia, Moravia, Austria, Germany, and Luxembourg were deported and resettled in the ghetto. The meeting of Eastern European Jews with those from Western Europe was a shock for both groups. The Western Jews, who had largely been assimilated, had difficulties finding a common language with the Jews of Lodz.

In order to accommodate them, Rumkowski ordered the closing of ghetto schools, and converted the schools into reception centers. The schools were never to open again.

In April 1942 Rumkowski issued orders requiring the unemployed, ten years old and up, to submit to examinations by a team of German doctors. Yet, those orders were not pursued. Instead, at the end of April, Rumkowski announced that the Western Jews would be deported, beginning on 4 May 1942, except for the employed among them and the holders of the Iron Cross or other World War I decorations. From 4 May to 15 May, 10,161 Central European Jews left Lodz in twelve transports to Chelmno. Even those eligible for exemption volunteered to leave, since the half-year they had spent in the ghetto, in hunger and cold, had deprived them of the will to live.

As Dawidowicz describes the tragedy:

> Where did they think they were going? At first, because their ghetto money was being changed into Reichsmarks, the deportees thought they were going to work in Germany. Others speculated that their destination was the General Government. People even heard rumors that the deportees had arrived in Warsaw. But the Lodz ghetto was so tightly sealed, a quarantined Jewish island in the hostile German land, that no news about Chelmno or Auschwitz seeped in. No one knew anything about the fate of the 55,000 deported Jews. (1975 : 293)

As a result of the Wannsee Conference on 20 January 1942, and its agreement on "the final solution of the Jewish question," orders for mass murders were issued. For the Lodz inhabitants the orders came in late summer 1942. During eight days of curfew between the fifth and twelfth of September 1942, known as the *groyse shpere* in Yiddish (Ger.: *Gesperre,* curfew), more than 20,000 sick, elderly, and children were sent to the Chelmno death camp. By the end of the first wave of extermination the Nazis had put more than 250,000 people to death. Those who remained in the ghetto lost any faith they may have had in Rumkowski's policy of appeasement.

During 1942, all the institutions of social welfare and public services, such as homes for the elderly, the orphanages, the hospitals, and the prayer houses, had been eliminated and their buildings or quarters turned into factories. The ghetto itself had been transformed into something like one great factory, with more than ninety enterprises employing over seventy-five thousand workers.

After the deportations of 1942, relative stability existed in Lodz. The ghetto's industry became useful for the Nazi war machine, and Nazi supervision of the ghetto was more evident than before. Many of Rumkowski's prerogatives were taken from him, and the administration offices were reduced or liquidated. The most important power of Rumkowski, the distribution of food, was taken over by Hans Biebow, the chief of the German ghetto administration, in October 1942. The *Sonderkommando*—a special unit of the *Ordnungsdienst* which was in charge of expropriations, operations against the black market, and political espionage—gained power due to its ties with the Germans. Rumkowski had to share his power with the Jewish police and the labor workshops managers.

In 1944, however, the Germans decided to liquidate the ghetto when Himmler instructed Arthur Greiser, the Nazi chief of Wartheland, to order deportations out of Lodz to Chelmno and Auschwitz. With the events of the war, the usefulness of this labor force became debatable, and on 15 June the Gestapo chief in Lodz, Bradfisch, informed Rumkowski that workers were needed inside Germany. The next day, the Eldest of the Jews issued a proclamation concerning voluntary registration of people to perform manual labor outside the ghetto. When there were too few volunteers, people were taken by force. Deportations to the death camps began a week later.

By the summer of 1944, the liquidation of the ghetto became total. Few people believed that they were going to work in Germany, as was announced. It was common knowledge that the Russians were only some 120 kilometers from Lodz, and many of the ghetto inhabitants did their best to postpone their departure by hiding. The Germans entered the ghetto armed with rifles and supplemented by the *Schutzpolizei* (German Protective Police Unit). They surrounded one block after the other, ordering the Jewish police, the *Sonder-*

kommando, to drag people out of hiding. By the time of the final *Gestapo* proclamation of 28 August 1944, the ghetto had already ceased to exist.

Among those on the last transport were Rumkowski, his wife, their adopted son, his brother, and his sister-in-law. They all apparently perished in Auschwitz-Birkenau sometime soon thereafter. The Jewish community of Lodz had been brought to an end.

Dawidowicz, in a long chapter titled "Death and Life in the East European Ghettos," summarizes this situation as follows: "The only institution comparable to the Nazi ghetto was the Nazi concentration camp. . . . Death bestrode the Nazi ghetto and was its true master, exercising its dominion through hunger, forced labor and disease" (1975 : 207).

Today, there are still eight open graves in the Jewish cemetery in Lodz; the Nazis had prepared them for the last of the Jews, who had remained behind to clean up the ghetto after the deportation of its populace. The forced march of the Germans from the city on 18 January 1945, in the face of the advancing Russian troops, prevented them from wiping out all traces of the ghetto before Lodz was liberated.

Some 877 people remained in the former area of the ghetto, left by the Nazis to carry out clean-up operations. Among them were those who found and safeguarded the ghetto archive's materials and documents, which included the *Chronicle of the Lodz Ghetto,* written by Alisha de Bunon, Julian Cukier, Shmul Hecht, Bernard Hellig, Abram Kamiencki, and others. This is a collective work which records the everyday life and events of the ghetto. Much of the information presented above is based on the *Chronicle* in its English version (1984), edited with an excellent foreword by Lucjan Dobroszycki, himself a survivor of the Lodz ghetto, and on the more detailed Hebrew version (in four volumes) translated and annotated by Arieh Ben-Menaḥem and Joseph Rab (1986–89).

Lodz: The Culture

Jews have been living in Poland since the thirteenth century. By World War II, there were 3,350,000 Jews in Poland (out of a total population of 27,000,000). They constituted this nation's largest ethnic group.

The cultural life of the Jews in the Lodz ghetto is but one chapter in the long and active history of Jews in Poland. However, because of the fate of the Jews of the Lodz ghetto (and others like it), many of the human as well as printed sources on the history of Polish Jewry have been destroyed. Modern scholarship often does disservice to the past creative culture of Polish Jewry by focusing exclusively on its destruction. This section, therefore, attempts to show how Jewish culture in the Lodz ghetto was, in modified form due to the oppressive historical context, a continuation of a creative and adaptive culture which existed before the war.[4]

"Like bread and potatoes, education and culture sustained life in the ghetto. The ghetto's taste in recreation ranged from low to high culture" (Dawidowicz 1975:255). In Lodz as in other ghettos, various cultural events took place, especially in the first years (1940 to 1942). All public events were supervised and censored by Rumkowski. After the *groyse shpere,* however, in which twenty thousand people were deported during an eight-day period, the ghetto's creative and spiritual sources were weakened, and most public performances came to an end.

Culture is inseparable from life. Thus, with the change of living conditions, the cultural context and content were changed as well. When Jewish holidays were forbidden to be observed in public, Jewish life-cycle ceremonies such as weddings became civil ceremonies and, with thc passing of time, rare occasions; the main stage for musicians and traditional entertainers was either dissolved or altered. Thus, the traditional entertainer-musician who was prominent before the war—the *badkhn* (wedding entertainer), the *klezmer* (instrumental musician), the *khazn* (cantor, sacred singer), and the *meshoyrer* (choirboy, cantor's assistant)—disappeared from the ghetto cultural life.

Instead, individual singers performed an eclectic repertoire conditioned by disparities in their early experience and modified by their ghetto experience. The individual singer of the ghetto is not different from prewar singers whose "repertoires were shaped by environment and acquisition patterns; they were not the same even among members of the same family, due to fluctuating social and economic situation and personal networks and affinities" (Slobin 1982:25).

With the rise of the Jewish Enlightenment (*Haskalah*) during the second half of the nineteenth century, a group of adventurous entertainers had begun to spread *Haskalah* songs in Yiddish. They performed on street corners and in wine cellars of Eastern Europe "with a new brand of lively, topical and satirical songs and skits tailored to an emerging middle class audience. . . . They were to form the nucleus of the movement toward a new Yiddish theater and to lay the groundwork for a whole new conception: the Yiddish popular song" (Slobin 1982:25). The popular Yiddish song was dominant in the ghetto. This ground of the popular Yiddish individual entertainer on the one hand, and the activities of the Yiddish theater troupes on the other, were modified in the ghetto and at the same time represented the stability of Yiddish popular music and its continuance.

As before the war, the variety of social movements, such as Zionism, Communism, and more, created new aspects of social organization and context along with a new repertoire of songs. Such movements before the war created workers' choruses, singing societies, and choirs such as the Lodz Hazamir (Heb.: The Nightingale), whose repertoire consisted largely of "national" Hebrew songs. In the ghetto, group performances within the ideological framework of the movement continued.

In addition, Jews performed in and attended the Polish (or other) concert halls and opera houses, which made them part of the "outside" culture yet influenced their own Jewish culture. This aspect of Jewish cultural life became an issue of emotional complexity during the war, as I will discuss later.

Cultural activity and events in the ghetto ranged from amateur and popular entertainment to professional performances, most of which were rooted in prewar Jewish cultural life. These activities can be divided into five types: 1. professional stage; 2. youth performance; 3. street entertainment; 4. amateur stage in the workplace; 5. domestic entertainment. The amateur stage performance was not based on any prewar tradition. It was a ghetto innovation reflecting the ghetto's central force: work. *The Chronicle of the Lodz Ghetto* reports on some of these events; others are mentioned in diaries or found their way into interviews with ghetto survivors.

Professional Stage

The *Chronicle* reports on several concerts and theater shows given in Lodz. For instance, on 1 March 1941, under the subtitle "cultural life," the *Chronicle* entry reads:

> Today the first symphonic concert conducted by David Beyglman took place in the auditorium of the House of Culture at 3 Krawiecka Street. The following works were performed: Bela Keler's overture, Popa's Suite Orientale and *Shabes nokh kugl* [After the Sabbath meal], Beyglman's *Wiegenlied* and *Chor der Derwische,* the overture from Massenet's *Phèdre,* Ayzenman's Jewish medleys, Siede's intermezzo, Shalit's *Der yosem* [The orphan] and *Ballet Orientale.* Accompanied by the orchestra, Mrs. [Ala] Diamant sang several soulful Yiddish songs. After the conclusion of the concert, Chairman Rumkowski addressed the audience on current affairs and his own plans. (Dobroszycki 1984:25)

In most of the concert programs given, the majority of works had Jewish overtones. David Beyglman (1887–1944), the usual conductor of these programs, was a professional musician attached to several Yiddish theater companies before his internment in Lodz. He was born into a musical family in Ostrowiec, in Kielce province. Like his brothers and sisters, he played many instruments, chiefly the clarinet and violin. In 1912, after his family moved to Lodz, he became director of the Yitskhok Zandberg Yiddish Theater Company. He was also connected in the 1920s with the other Yiddish theaters, Azazel and Ararat, both active in Lodz. In August 1944, he was deported to Auschwitz.

Rumkowski spoke at the conclusion of every concert. His presence added a political dimension to the shows, thus not allowing the audience to escape completely their harsh environment.

Concert programs took place at the House of Culture. This hall contained four hundred seats and was well equipped with professional stage equipment, lighting, and so on. In addition to having the ghetto's symphony orchestra, the hall provided a venue for the Lodz Choral Society Hazamir as well as the Revue Theater. The latter was like its American counterpart, a musical theater of a fast, smart, and topical nature (Hamm 1979: 132).

The traumatic deportations of September 1942 can be detected by reading between the lines of the *Chronicle* entry for 7 November 1942:

> Today, after an interval of over two months, a concert once again took place in the House of Culture. Conducted by David Beyglman, the program consisted of his latest compositions, nearly all of them concerto fantasies and variations on popular Jewish themes. . . . Since its concertmaster has died, the orchestra was incomplete, and a few of its members, for example, Professor Wachtel (viola), have been resettled. Now, the musicians can play only in their spare time, since the House of Culture no longer exists as an independent department and all musicians are employed in workshops or departments. After the concert, the Chairman delivered a speech. . . . [He] announced, regular concerts will again be performed from now on. (Dobroszycki 1984: 287)

Indeed, another concert conducted by David Beyglman and concluded by Rumkowski is mentioned on 14 November 1942 (Dobroszycki 1984: 289). The final concert to be reported took place on 6 December 1942 (Dobroszycki 1984: 296).

The last performance with Beyglman conducting was noted on 8 March 1944; this was his "farewell" concert. On this occasion he was not leading the orchestra but conducting

> the surrender of musical instruments: . . . The [German] expert asked Beyglman about the value and quality of the instruments, and Beyglman attempted to explain the special qualities of each item. But [the expert], . . . showed little comprehension of the various treasures and set prices that sounded like jokes. . . . The finest instruments purchased from the Jews went to the Reich's Chamber of Music for the following sums: fifteen master violins . . . for a total of 100 Marks (roughly seven Marks apiece), two master saxophones . . . for 40 Marks, four pianos, all of them first-rate makes and nearly new, with a total value of approximately 7,000 Marks, were bought from the Jews by the expert for a total of 600 Marks. Splendid mandolins, guitars, zithers, lutes, flutes, saxophones, trumpets, cymbals and so forth, were assigned an average price of 2 or 3 Marks apiece. (Dobroszycki 1984 : 471)

The detailed list of instruments and their prices summarizes the life and death of musical performances in Lodz. Music could be performed as long as permission was granted and the physical conditions of the ghetto permitted it. When there were no performers and nothing to eat, instruments had to be converted into money or food.

Theater performances took place even before the opening of the House of Culture and its symphonic music events. Moishe Pulaver (born 1902, Lodz) established a theater troupe in the summer of 1940 under the name Avantgarde. Before the war he was the director of the Lodz Yiddish theater Ararat. In August 1944 he was deported to Auschwitz; from there he was sent to a labor camp in Germany. He was liberated from this labor camp in 1945. In his memoirs[5] Pulaver describes a rich theatrical life in Lodz before the war, including local theater companies and visiting theaters such as the Vilna Troupe and Habimah. The variety of theater companies and the frequent attendance made the audience of Lodz a *meyvn* (Yidd.: critical expert) (Pulaver 1963 : 57).

The premiere performance of the Ghetto Theater was at the sports hall of the ghetto's gymnasium. Rumkowski was not in attendance; however, his confederates informed him that the performance was "acceptable." Permission was given to continue the shows in the House of Culture before its official opening as such; this time Rumkowski did attend.

When Rumkowski was present at the first performance in the new location on 24 October 1940, he disapproved of two sketches which he thought too critical, and ordered the theater closed. Later, he gave permission to have the theater reopened for two shows twice a week. The official troupe which operated the theater consisted of eighteen actors; seven dancers; a choir; a painter/set designer/cho-

Moishe Pulaver, the director, and the writer Jachimowitz with the cast of *Yidn Schmidn* (Jewish Blacksmith). Zonabend Collection, YIVO Institute for Jewish Research.

reographer, Pinchas Shaar (Schwartz) (b. 1917; his story will be introduced later in this work); and a music director, David Beyglman.

These shows proved extremely popular and the songs introduced in the revue immediately became ghetto hits. As in every revue theater performance of that time, "the success of the show depended on the songs" (Hamm 1979: 133). Eighty-five shows were produced in the House of Culture from its opening until the end of 1941, with more than seventy thousand people attending.

The *Chronicle* reports on a 31 May premiere of a revue, giving a short description of the show's character and the talent behind it:

> The show was composed of skits, genre pieces touching on current events, monologues, and dance performers. Considering the conditions of ghetto life and the lack of professional performers, the revue surpassed all expectations. This show can, without reservation, be ranked with those put on stage by good pre-war theaters. The revue's success is due to its director, Mr. [Moishe] Pulaver, to the author of many of the more successful pieces, [Shimon] Yanovsky, and to the truly masterful sets produced by the painter [Pinchas] Schwartz. The revue was performed entirely in Yiddish. The audience at Saturday's premier demanded encores for several numbers with thunderous ap-

> plause. After the performance Chairman Rumkowski delivered a lengthy speech. . . . (Dobroszycki 1984:57–58)

Throughout the turbulent times of the ghetto, the theater represented normalcy and the continuity of Yiddish tradition. In 1942, the last full year the theater was permitted to operate, 105 shows were produced, drawing an audience of 45,000. Naturally, attendance decreased with the population of the ghetto. And all performances were heavily censored, monitored, and hastily rewritten, if necessary, under the authoritarian eye of Rumkowski and his aides.

The House of Culture was officially closed in the summer of 1942 and set up to be a factory for blankets and pillows; the revue shows were discontinued that same summer.

Youth Performance

The *Chronicle* for 6 September 1941 records:

> A show entitled *A Summer Holiday* was staged by the Marysin administration at the House of Culture. The cast of the program, which lasted several hours, was composed exclusively of children who were at Marysin to study or to rest. The program included choral singing, recitations, vignettes of the children's lives in Marysin, dance, farces, and so on. As a whole it was truly impressive. The children displayed genuine talent in all their performances. Guests present by invitation filled every seat and the community's administration was fully represented. At the end of this pleasant entertainment, the Chairman delivered a short speech. . . . After the Chairman's speech, the little children made a ring around him on the stage and danced joyously accompanied by the sound of music and cheers for the ghetto's first citizen. The Chairman gave a present of bread and candy to each of the show's young performers. (Dobroszycki 1984:75)

Rumkowski took a special interest in the welfare of the orphans of Lodz, perhaps because he had no children of his own. He personally supervised the orphanage, located in Marysin, and it was perhaps as a tribute to "the leader" that a group of counselors staged the first theatrical productions. The shows proved exceptionally popular, and several of them were repeated at the House of Culture.

Dramatic societies also thrived among the various ghetto youth organizations; some of them had a *Kibbutz*-like setup located in Marysin. Performances took place regularly on Friday afternoons (before the Sabbath) and the Jewish holidays, as well as on special occasions such as the name-days of important Zionist and youth organization leaders.

Following the *groyse shpere,* too few youth remained to perform or make up an audience. Thus, the various forms of organized youth entertainment came to an end. Those children who remained were sent to the workshops where some of them participated in various adult theatrical and musical performances.

Although organized performances of the children ended, the *Chronicle* reports on a castanetlike toy instrument some children invented. Following a detailed description of this instrument, the chronicler, Oskar Rosenfeld, remarks (in the entry of 25 August 1943):

> The instrument imposes no limit on the individual's musical ability. . . . The streets of Litzmannstadt ghetto are filled with clicking, drumming, banging. . . . Barefoot boys scurry past you, performing their music right under your nose, with great earnestness, as though their lives depended on it. Here the musical instinct of Eastern European Jews is cultivated to the full. An area that has given the world so many musicians, chiefly violinists—just think of Hubermann, Heifetz, Elman, Milstein, Menuhin—now presents a new line of artists. . . . A few boys gathered, clicked their castanets, and all hell let loose. It was the first castanet concert I had ever attended. (Dobroszycki 1984:374)

Thus "high culture" becomes popular culture, and the theater stage is replaced by the ghetto streets. The tragedy of the youth emerges, and yet there is hope.

Street Entertainment

Street entertainment was known in Lodz as well as in other cities in Poland before the war. In public gardens, street corners, backyards of houses, and other places, singers, musicians, and jugglers performed. They tried their best to attract attention from passersby, sitting at their windows and hoping to collect some pennies in their hats. Roving bands of Jewish musicians and traveling individual singers have been known in Poland since the eighteenth century. The *Haskalah* singer gained popularity in Eastern Europe in the early twentieth century and found a fertile ground and a captive audience in the ghetto.

A few months after the ghetto was sealed, public transportation ceased operating, and people were out of work. Yet with their money still valid, they flocked to the traffic-free city streets.

No one now can estimate the number of street performers active in the ghetto from the very beginning; nor are many of them remembered by name. Yet every survivor has a vivid recollection of these performers, and such recollections contribute to the story of singing in the ghetto. The performers' names may not be important, but the songs they sang are.

Yaakov Flam (b. 1930, Lodz) recalls a diminutive street singer who performed along with an accompanying violinist. He claims that even at that time he thought that the short man who sang in the streets was "a genius." He also remembers two orphan children, whose names he does not remember, but thinks they were among those children brought into the ghetto from Germany.

Yaakov Rotenberg (b. 1926, Lodz), who discussed street performances with me, also remembers seeing that short man. According to Rotenberg, this man stood on a stool, and raised his hand in a call for revolt while singing. The man then moved on to the next corner, where he began his performance over again.

Arieh Ben-Menaḥem (b. 1922, Lodz) claims that there were two street singers in the ghetto: Yankele Hershkowitz and "Kleine Yidele" (Yidd.: the little Jew). Yankele Hershkowitz was a man of average height, and Kleine Yidele, short. Pinchas Shaar (Schwartz) (b. 1917, Lodz), on the other hand, remembers only Yankele Hershkowitz, describing him as a short man who always carried a stool to stand on while singing in the streets, thus claiming that Yankele Hershkowitz was also known as Kleine Yidele.

Most entertainers, while able to draw a crowd, could not collect enough money on which to survive. Thus, one by one, they vanished until but a single performer, a "voice of the ghetto," remained: Yankele Hershkowitz. A short, heavy man, who stood on a stool to perform, and who was sometimes accompanied by the Viennese violinist Karl Rosentsweig, Hershkowitz composed songs that commented on the ongoing events with satire and humor. Not much is known of Hershkowitz's personal life. According to Yeḥiel Frenkiel, however, he survived the war and remained in Poland, where he died (by his own hand) in the 1970s.

During his internment in Lodz, Yeḥiel Frenkiel's father, Shlomo Frank (Frenkiel), kept a diary which mentions Yankele several times. In a late entry he writes how Yankele once approached him and asked for his assistance with Yiddish writing. (Frank was a well-known journalist.) Frank demurred: "Why don't you ask Jachimowitz or Graf-Kali?" (These were famous poets resident in the ghetto.) Yankele replied, "They get angry at me, they think that I am not a poet but a crazy man. But in these days in the ghetto do you have to be a talented poet? You need but some rhymes and to sing" (Frank 1958:370).

Most of the survivors I interviewed recall street songs and attribute them to "Yankele." The ghetto literary Hebrew newspaper *Min Hametsar,* however, mentions another singer in addition to Yankele, named "Dasao." *Min Hametsar,* in fact, regularly published a section on "songs of the ghetto," acknowledging the importance of collecting and disseminating this material (Blumental 1951 : 115–83). In one such column, titled "The poets of the ghetto—the short black Jew" (in Yiddish, *dos shvartse yidele*), the journalist writes:

> . . . the short black Jew who stands on a box surrounded by hundreds of listeners is like an endless gusher. Every day he pours forth a new song. He sings his songs and they immediately become the subject of the day or the song of the day. What doesn't he sing about? He sings of the Nine Marks [the amount given to the unemployed to obtain their food] and of the police. And the police themselves stand and listen to this critique; they do not comment but enjoy the fact that they have become the subject of the nation's spirit, and gain immortality through everlasting songs. Once upon a time, a policeman wanted to arrest the poet because he insulted the Eldest [Rumkowski]. The crowd surrounded the poet and would not let the policeman get close enough to arrest him. The poet was set free. After every song he cries out: "a new song for ten Pfennig and no more." The crowd searches throughout their pockets, and one by one they collect the sum of ten Pfennig. Then, our poet continues, and so on. (*Min Hametsar,* 8 July 1941, in Blumental 1951 : 134–35)

Whatever their number, the street singers were a movable cabaret, offering social and political satire, humor and parodies of popular songs in response to the daily life in the ghetto. They sang for an audience hungry not only for bread and potatoes, but also for freedom of expression.

The Amateur Stage in the Workplace

The first public shows in the workplaces occurred in the public kitchens, which functioned as the main attraction in the streets of the ghetto. The *Chronicle* entry has the following information from 1 March 1941: "There were performances by the violinist Miss Bronislawa Rotshtat in the hall at Soup Kitchen No. 2 [for the intelligentsia], and, as usual, it met with great success. Teodor Ryder [1881–1944, piano] accompanied. [Nickodem] Shtayman enchanted the audience with his pleasant tenor. Today, on the premises of the [labor Zionist soup kitchen] at [10] Masarska Street the fifth consecutive *Oyneg Shabes* [Joy of Sabbath] evening took place and was dedicated to recitations and songs" (Dobroszycki 1984 : 25).

The comment on the audience reflects the fact that even within the ghetto, class and status were determined by wealth, occupation, education, and family (Dawidowicz 1975:213). Even in Lodz, the city of blue-collar workers, the intelligentsia retained prestige, at least in the early years.

In the workshops, known in Lodz as *Ressorts* (Ger.: workplace), workers created shows for their coworkers and put on performances for special occasions. Children took part in some of these shows. The revue shows included sketches and songs and dealt with life in the workplace. After the *groyse shpere,* which ended the professional stage performances, the youth organization performances, and the street entertainment, the workshops became the main stage for the ghetto's cultural life. Events occasionally included guest shows by performers from other workshops. At the beginning of 1943 the workshops celebrated their first, second, or even third anniversaries, during which revue performances took place either in the workshops or at the former House of Culture.

The paper factory, for example, with more than a thousand workers, staged the largest revue show, with seventy people taking part. This particular show was performed four times, and people from other workshops came to see it; Rumkowski also attended and gave presents to the participants.

In the first revue show of anniversary events on 1 April 1943, the "Vegetable Department" performed a satirical song on the *Sonderkommando* (see discussion of song 4). Gertler, chief of the *Sonderkommando,* was in the audience and decreed this song not be performed again. Following the incident, Rumkowski ordered that every piece be approved by him personally before its performance.

On 20 June 1943, Moishe Pulaver, the former director of the Avantgarde Theater, directed the "Shoe *Ressort*" show, which included parts to be performed by children, and these last were the success of the evening. The music was composed by David Beyglman, who also conducted the choir (Pulaver 1963:15–17).

Such shows were the final organized music-theater productions performed in the ghetto. On 21 June 1943, Rumkowski decreed that there would be no more performances, possibly because one of the pieces performed that evening seemed to be critical of his authority. But although public shows were forbidden, artistic activity continued in the workshops: poetry readings, recitations, dance performances, sketches, and monologues narrating life in the workplaces continued almost until the ghetto's final liquidation.[6]

Domestic Entertainment

Although forbidden officially, the Jewish holidays were celebrated at home, with singing around tables devoid of traditional—or indeed any—food. Birthday celebrations occurred very rarely, while marriage and *Bar Mitzvah* ceremonies included usually the necessary blessings but were not followed by the traditional celebration. If it proved possible, the ceremony was followed by a small reception which could include some singing but definitely no dancing.

Lucille Eichengreen (b. 1925, Hamburg) recalls two or three chamber music concerts in private homes in the latter part of 1942. She remembers the performance of a violin, viola, and another string instrument: "We sat on the floor. I think the music was Mozart. . . . It was not what you would call a professional performance, but it was music. It was something that did not exist otherwise in the ghetto, it was remarkable. It made us think that there was still hope. After the performance the small audience had to stay overnight because of the curfew."

She also speaks of an evening organized by one of her office mates in 1943, in which one of the coworkers sang some Yiddish songs written by Isaiah Shpigl (1906–90, a poet and a writer who worked at that office); this was followed by a dance: "Someone brought records and an old-fashioned wind-up record player and the dances were mainly tangos. The audience was only from the office, about twenty to thirty people, and it happened only twice."

Esther Milch (b. 1920, Pyontek) recollects reading aloud for a group of ten people who came to hear her, since she managed to keep her books after the ghetto was sealed. Miriam Harel remembers reading aloud her own poetry, sometimes set to adapted melodies, performing at home for her family, as I shall present later in this work.

Shlomo Flam (b. 1922, Lodz) remembers his nineteenth birthday party at his parents' home in the ghetto. To this unusual occasion he invited his friends from the Gordonya Youth Organization as well as some family members. The party took place in the evening during the blackout. Group singing of Hebrew songs comprised the evening's artistic program. This is a case in which the context (domestic) and the content (youth organization) do not coincide. This example points out the variety of cultural activities, and the problems of categorization. However, even in this mixed case, the context should be dominant in defining the culture, and thus this event is included here.

Birthday party for Shlomo Flam (center), March 1941, in the ghetto. Shlomo Flam Collection.

When survivors recall their experiences in the ghetto, they first recall the suffering, the abnormal everyday life they led. This is what seems most important to them. Yet almost every survivor I interviewed also recalled some kind of domestic entertainment: singing, reading aloud, recitations, or prayer. These activities had a comforting effect on them and represented normalcy to them.

NOTES

1. Interview with Miriam Harel, Kiryat Bialik, 2 August 1986.

2. Chelmno, only thirty-one miles from Lodz, was the first camp to use gas vans. The vans went into operation five weeks before the Wannsee Conference.

3. The sources for the dates and figures were compiled by Marek Web in a recent bibliography, *The Documents of the Lodz Ghetto—An Inventory of the Nachman Zonabend Collection* (New York: 1988).

4. Aleksander Hertz's *The Jews in Polish Culture* (translated edition 1988) is the only available source in English on the topic. The book was written in 1963 from a Polish Jewish perspective; it focused on the image of Jews in the eyes of the non-Jews, which is out of the scope for my discussion. Besides, Hertz devotes only one page to the role of Jewish musicians in Polish folk music, on which he calls for more research (1988 : 132–33).

5. Moishe Pulaver published his memoirs in Yiddish, *Geven iz a geto* (There was a ghetto) (Tel Aviv: 1963). His career with the Ararat theater is described in his book of essays devoted to prewar characters in Lodz titled *Ararat un Lodzer typn* (Ararat and Lodz characters) (Tel Aviv: 1972).

6. This section is partially based on Frenkiel 1986a: 12–43.

2

Chaim Rumkowski: The Man and the Song

Of all the songs sung in the ghetto, one stands out in the survivors' memory: "Rumkowski Chaim." The song concerns the dominant figure in the ghetto, Chaim Rumkowski, head of the Jewish Council, and dubbed the Eldest of the Jews. Though he did not survive the war, the recollections and song that lived after him testify to his importance.

Although a discussion of Rumkowski's role in the ghetto appeared to the previous chapter, and the discussion of the "hit song" could comprise the beginning of the next chapter (dealing with street songs), I devote this chapter to the man and the song. I do this in response to the sources I have examined and the testimonies I have recorded from survivors. All sources focus on the visible power in the ghetto reflected in Mordechai Chaim Rumkowski.[1] The questions of how much power and control of ghetto life he really had serving under Nazi terror, what he knew about the fate of the deported Jews, and whether his ghetto policy was right prompt endless discussion among scholars, survivors, and others. It is beyond the scope of my study to participate in this discussion, thus I make a point of portraying the man from both the historical perspective and the artistic outlook as a central figure, the principal actor in the ghetto streets—the ghetto stage.

The Man: King of the Ghetto

A German document signed by City Commissioner Leiser on 13 October 1939 states:

> The Eldest of the Jews in the City of Lodz, Rumkowski has been named to implement all orders by the German Civil Administration of the city of Lodz concerning persons of Jewish race. He is personally

Chaim Rumkowski (center) and members of the *Sonderkommando.* Zonabend Collection, YIVO Institute for Jewish Research.

> responsible to me in this connection. To implement these tasks, he is entitled to 1. Move freely in the streets at any hour, day and night; 2. Have access to the offices of the German administration; 3. Choose a Council of Elders and to confer with them; 4. Use wall posters to announce his orders; 5. Control the assembly of Jewish labor detachments. Every person of Jewish race is obliged to absolutely obey all of the Eldest Rumkowski's orders. Opposition to him will be punished by me. (Adelson and Lapides 1989 : 19)

There are various explanations of how and why Rumkowski was nominated to this position. A childless widower and the director of an orphanage, he had been elected to the Lodz *kehilla* (Heb.: Jewish community; before the war, the name of the Jewish community's council) on the Zionist ticket. When the Germans burst into the *kehilla* offices in October 1939 and asked for the *Altester,* Rumkowski, then sixty-two years old, responded, thinking they meant "oldest," not "Eldest," an honorific for council leader, whom they wanted to appoint. Another story has it that on learning that the

Germans were trying to locate *kehilla* officers, Rumkowski voluntarily reported and offered his services. And yet another version has it that he was selected because of his noble appearance. None of these accounts can be substantiated (Dobroszycki 1984: xliv and n. 118).

Rumkowski was not an exception in proceeding directly from the *kehilla* board to the Jewish Council, the *Judenrat*.[2] Following his nomination on 13 October 1939, Rumkowski had been ordered to select a Council of Elders, known as the *Beirat*. All but eight of its thirty members were arrested on 7 November 1939, taken away, and killed less than a month after their selection.

Three months later, on 5 February 1940, the nomination of a new twenty-one member *Beirat* was announced by Rumkowski. The Germans, however, treated it as a mere formality. Rumkowski became in effect the sole ruler of the Lodz ghetto. One man was sufficient for the Germans in Lodz, and it did not matter who he was as long as he was obedient, able to maintain order in the Jewish quarter, and could mobilize people for work.

Rumkowski took his appointment as Eldest of the Jews very seriously, although it is difficult to assume that he considered it a step forward socially or politically. According to Dobroszycki (1984: xlvi–xlvii), it is also unlikely that Rumkowski accepted the post in the hope of gaining material or personal advantage. To deal with the affairs of a community seemed to be his calling, and with the outbreak of the war his activities in the field and sense of his own importance grew considerably.

Rumkowski approached the German authorities with a proposition to use the ghetto's manpower to manufacture goods for the Germans in exchange for food. The Germans accepted his proposition and the Chairman began to register workers, build workshops, and negotiate the exchange of products for food. He was well aware of what the Nazis were capable of doing, but believed that with obedient behavior on the part of the Jews, things could be worked out. His credo throughout the ghetto period was "calm and work": by "calm" he meant obedience to his authority; by "work" he meant making the ghetto indispensable to the German war machine.

Rumkowski addressed the ghetto inhabitants very often in public speeches and printed announcements in a patronizing way, the way he had spoken to his helpless orphans: "Jews, remain calm. I will do everything possible and I will endeavor most energetically to carry out my tasks" (Announcement no. 104, 12 August 1940, in Adelson and Lapides 1989: 92–93).

Obedience and work would keep the Jews alive until the end of the war, and his slogan made sense in the early period of the ghetto. Rumkowski maintained that conviction until the very end, even when he realized that ghetto inhabitants were being deported to death camps.

Rumkowski's rule can be divided into two periods. In the early part of the war he acted forcefully, efficiently, and speedily to establish a well-run ghetto empire: workshops, police, courts of justice, jails, and schools. To visit the various departments, he traveled in a horse-drawn carriage donated by the Germans. He supervised workers in the public kitchens as they doled out soup to the starving population and checked on the food stores.

Rumkowski spoke ironically about the Warsaw *Judenrat,* which he had visited. In Warsaw, he said, chaos reigned—children were dying in the streets while food was plentiful in elegant cafes and restaurants. In actual fact, starvation in Lodz was even worse than in Warsaw; in the latter, smugglers brought in food and other essential products from the outside with the support of the Jewish authorities. Lodz, on the other hand, was a completely isolated ghetto. The difference, however, was that while in Warsaw the dead lay on the streets for a long time before they were buried, in Lodz burial took place almost immediately.

Some Lodz inhabitants, including members of Rumkowski's administration, agreed with his strategies; but others frequently rebelled. When a "go-slow" movement began in the workshops, Rumkowski spread rumors among the workers that would either calm them down or threaten them with reprisals. Order was maintained by any and all means. To silence his opponents he used the threat of unemployment, starvation, and finally deportation.

The situation changed, however, when in mid-1942 Rumkowski realized that Jews were being murdered. In deep pain Rumkowski asked the inhabitants to deliver twenty thousand of the sick, the elderly, and children on 5 September 1942. After the eight-day curfew known as the *groyse shpere,* the quota was delivered. Rumkowski addressed the remaining ghetto population and ordered them to work: "Here in the ghetto we are all workers, we are all equal!" (from Rumkowski's speech of November 1942, in Adelson and Lapides 1989: 373). Rumkowski did not change his policy and continued to obey Nazi orders, believing that by sacrificing some he could save many others.

Rumkowski was the one to determine which of the ghetto's remaining 60,000 to 70,000 Jews should die and which should live, until he was deported in August of 1944. Sixty thousand people died in the ghetto, whether from starvation, freezing, disease, hanging, or suicide. From the ghetto, 130,000 who were deported died either in the exhaust vans at Chelmno or the gas chambers of Auschwitz.

Rumkowski's strategy was almost successful. The Lodz ghetto was the last one to remain in existence in Poland. However, when the Germans proceeded to the final solution, "productivity" ceased to be a consideration and thus no longer any help.

In August 1944 the Nazis sent Rumkowski and most of the ghetto inhabitants to Auschwitz-Birkenau. There are several accounts of how Rumkowski perished, but all versions note that he was "welcomed" with great hatred by his fellow Jews from Lodz who were already in Auschwitz. In one account, Rumkowski was beaten to death by Jews from the ghetto who were awaiting his arrival. His body was then thrown into an open pit where bodies were burned. A second account describes Rumkowski's arrival at Auschwitz with his young wife and their adopted son. He presented a letter of introduction provided to him in Lodz by Hans Biebow. He was welcomed on the platform and told he would be given a tour of the facility. But he was brought instead to the crematorium. He and his family were burned alive without being gassed. The last account has it that Rumkowski was separated for his age and put to death in due course. As with the accounts of the "king's" nomination, none of the accounts of the "king's" death could be substantiated (Adelson and Lapides 1989: 493–99).

Would Rumkowski have been vindicated after the war for saving Jewish lives, or would he have been condemned as the murderer of tens of thousands? Survivors have asked themselves this question for four decades. It would seem a moral issue difficult or even impossible to resolve.

The Song: A "Hit"

During the first year of the ghetto's existence the song "Rumkowski Chaim," performed by the street entertainer Yankele Hershkowitz, became very popular. Most of the survivors remember the song, even if they do not recall the singer's real name and do not remember seeing him in the ghetto.

Yankele Hershkowitz and his "hit song" are described by the chroniclers in their entry of 5 December 1941:

Yankele Hershkowitz performs in the street, accompanied by Karl Rosentsweig. Zonabend Collection, YIVO Institute for Jewish Research.

The author and performer of this song is the popular ghetto street "troubadour" (Yankele) Hershkowitz, formerly a tailor by trade. Last year he composed the extremely popular topical song entitled "Rumkowski Chaim" . . . and once even received a gift of five Marks from the Chairman himself, who had chanced to hear the song. Another time, the ghetto "troubadour" received a package of *matzoth* from the Chairman in person when he was performing his song in front of a store which the Chairman happened to be visiting before the holidays. At present the song writer has formed a partnership with a man from Vienna, a certain Karl Rosentsweig, a former traveling salesman. Rosentsweig accompanies Hershkowitz on the guitar or zither. And this duo, which, like everything else in the ghetto, is a bit peculiar, being composed of a tailor from Bałut and a traveling salesman from Vienna, is enjoying great success with the populace. This is of course good for their business and the duo sometimes ends up with six Marks to share after a full day's work, a tidy wage indeed. The partnership has recently launched a new song.[3] . . . The ghetto's songwriter also composed another very popular "hit song" entitled "lebn zol prezes Chaim" (Long live Chairman Chaim). (Dobroszycki 1984:92)

Yankele Hershkowitz composed and sang his songs in Yiddish, the Jewish vernacular. The verses covered a broad range of political and social topics in which the singer lamented the past and commented on the present. He continued the tradition of the *broder-singers* (singers from Brody) of the *Haskalah* period, the wandering minstrels who entertained on the street corners of Eastern Europe with topical and satirical songs. However, unlike his predecessors who traveled from one town to the next, the ghetto singer was confined to the ghetto.

Yankele Hershkowitz could also be classified as a typical Eastern European Yiddish folk singer, one of those performers of the last two centuries who later became popular singers in the growing urban centers of Poland and elsewhere. According to Cahan, one of the early folklorists of Jewish folksong, such a singer came from a low- to middle-class family and used his talent to earn additional income. Due to his background, his repertoire addressed the issues of "all people," and he drew on familiar topics and musical sources: "his outlook of the world is the same as that of his fellow men, he draws his ideas from the common life of his surroundings, using the folk's mouth and his own soul. He is one of the masses with a natural poetic nature, but not a famous [literate] poet" (Cahan 1952: 11).

The Jewish folksinger of the interwar period was exposed to both Yiddish and Polish folk music and popular music, as well as to American popular music, both Jewish and non-Jewish, which made its way to Europe. In addition, the singer could be exposed to classical music or its popular rendition and to Jewish sacred music. The main difference that separated the Jewish singer from his neighbors before 1939 was his use of two internal languages: Yiddish and Hebrew.

Thus the description of Yankele Hershkowitz given by Rachmil Bryks in his novel *Di papirene kroyn* (The paper crown) fits into the framework of the typical Jewish folksinger:

> Yankele was a genuine folksinger. . . . Just before World War II he arrived in Lodz from Aft. He was a tailor of cheap designs, a simple, nice man. All his education came from the *kheyder* where he studied *'vry* [the basic Hebrew alphabet and biblical stories]. . . . At a young age he had to go to work to help his poor family. He did not even know Polish; he wrote Yiddish with mistakes. . . . He traveled with other tailors to nearby towns to trade his merchandise and thus he learned folksongs and folktales. . . . He had a pleasant voice. He enjoyed singing and sang very emotionally. For each event of the *shtetl* he com-

> posed a poem and adapted it to a well-known melody. Soon afterwards, all the people of the *shtetl* sang his rhymes. . . . When the ghetto was sealed and Yankele did not have anything on which to survive, he knew that Mordechai Chaim Rumkowski was responsible for that; and this was what most of the ghetto inhabitants thought. . . . Thus he composed the song about Rumkowski . . . and adapted the lyrics to an old folk melody. . . . (1969:34–35)

In the ghetto, where no radios were allowed, newspapers forbidden, and political gatherings outlawed, the only form of expression still permitted (albeit supervised) was singing. Thus, it is not surprising that the "king of the ghetto"—Chaim Rumkowski—became the theme of "Rumkowski Chaim," a song that was to be the ghetto's greatest "hit."

Yankele Hershkowitz was accompanied, some survivors observe, by a musical instrument. However, there is some debate over the instrument used. The conflicting reports prove one thing at any rate: his accompaniment was most likely an ad-hoc affair determined by the availability of instruments and accompanists.

Hershkowitz uses a verse-refrain structure for this song as well as for most of his songs. These are most likely contrafact, that is, songs created by setting new words to a pre-existing melody, a method traditional among folk poets who are also folksingers. According to Beregovski, the "new" satirical songs "largely use the devices of contrast and parody, as did the older satirical songs . . ." (1982:34). My research has not yielded an original source for the melody of "Rumkowski Chaim," and it is more than likely that Hershkowitz drew his melody from the body of Yiddish folk tunes.

The version I present here is one I recorded in Israel during the summer of 1985.[4] It was sung by Yaakov Rotenberg, a survivor of the Lodz ghetto who was fourteen when the ghetto was sealed. The text is transcribed into Latin characters according to the pronunciation of the informant in his special Lodz dialect. An English translation is provided along with the Yiddish. (The words in the lyrics which are marked with an asterisk are discussed in note 4.)

Song 1

Rumkovski khayim (Rumkowski Chaim)

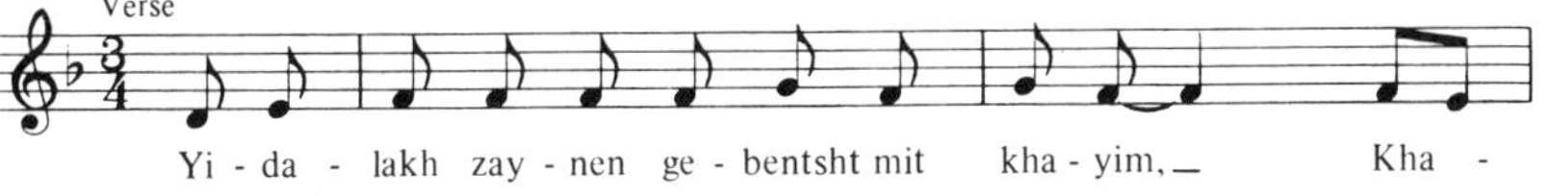

yim le - oy - lam mu - ves, Kha - yim fin beys ha - kha - yim,
Rum-kov-ski kha-yim mit zayn groy - sn nes. Er makht dekh
ni - sim oy, Yey-dn tug a - zoy, Ge - valt tsi shra - a - yen oy, oy,
oy, Ye-der ay - ner frey - gt A tsvay - te shay -
le, oy. Zugt er kha - yim s'iz git a - zoy.
Refrain
Vayl ind - zer kha - yim, Er get indz kla - yen, Er get indz
gro - pn, Er get indz man, Far-tsay - tns hobn di mid - ber yi - dn
ge - ge - sn man; Hay - nt est shoyn ye - de vayb ir
man. Rum-kov-ski kha - yim hot git ge - trakht, Ge - ar - bet
shve - [e] r bay tug bay nakht, Ge-makht a ge - to in a
dye - to, In er shrayt ge - vald ar iz ge - rakht!

Verse 1:
Yidalakh zaynen gebentsht mit khayim,
Khayim leoylam muves,
Khayim fin beys ha'khayim,
Rumkovski khayim mit zayn groysn nes.
Er makht dekh nisim oy,
Yeydn tug azoy,
Gevalt tsi shrayen oy, oy, oy,
Yeyder ayner freygt:
A tsvayte shayle, oy,
Zugt er khayim s'iz git azoy!

Refren:
Vayl [er iz] indzer khayim,
Er get indz klayen,
Er get indz gropn,
Er get indz man.*
Fartsaytns hobn di midber yidn gegesn man;
Haynt est shoyn yede vayb ir man.
Rumkovski khayim hot git getrakht,
Gearbet shver bay tug bay nakht,
Gemakht a geto in a dyeto
In er shrayt gevald a[z] [e]r iz gerakht!

Verse 2:
Khayim vaytsman hot gezugt:
Az er vil di yidn in palestine hobn.
Hot zay gehaysn akern zeyen,
Er hot zay dortn tif bagrubn;
Ober indzer khayim'l,
Rumkovski khayim,
Er get indz yeydn tug shrayim:
Aynem a shtik broyt,
In tsveytn a shtik ferd,
Me leygt bay eyem oyekh tif'n drerd.

Refren: Vayl iz indzer . . .

Verse 3:
Der driter khayim fin beys ha'khayim,
Hot mit malkhe [ha]muves a git gesheft gemakht:
Er zol im tsishteln maysim vus mer;
Er zol im tsishteln bay tug bay nakht.
Hot zekh der malekh ha'muves genimen
Tsi der arbet shnel.
Er makht fin yedn giber* oy a tel:
Er makht des flink,
Er makht des git.
Er makht di gantse geto* shvakh in mid.

Refren: Vayl iz indzer . . .

Verse 4:
In a zimer tug,
Geveyzn iz a tug a hayser,
Geyt rumkovski in der gas,
Er zet dokh oys vi a keyser.
A hele antsug, oy,
In tinkele briln,
Politsay arim bevakht.
Iekh zug aykh guer
Indzer keyser hot groue huer;
Leybn zol er gantse hindert yuer!

Refren: Vayl iz indzer . . .

Verse 5:
Rumkovski khayim der eltster yude,
Iz ungeshtelt bay di gestapo.
Meye yidalakh zaynen zayne bruder,
In er farzorgt indz di papo.
Er makht dekh nisim oy,
Yeydn tug azoy
Gevald tsi shrayen oy, oy, oy!
Yeyder ayner freygt:
A tsvayte shayle oy?
Zugt er khayim: s'iz git azoy!

Verse 1:
Jews are seen to be blessed with life,
Life until death,
Life from the house of life,
Rumkowski Chaim and his great miracle.
He makes miracles, oy,
So every day,
For heaven's sake, oy, oy, oy,
Everyone asks:
A second question, oy?
Chaim says: It's good this way!

Refrain:
Because [he is] our Chaim*
He gives us bran,
He gives us barley,
He gives us manna.*
Once upon a time Jews of the desert ate manna;
Now each woman eats her husband.
Rumkowski Chaim thought it through,

Worked hard day and night,
Made a ghetto with a diet (store),*
And claims gevald that he is right!

Verse 2:
Chaim Weizmann said:
He wants to have the Jews in Palestine.
He told them to plow, sow,
He did them in there deep;
But, our Chaim,
Rumkowski Chaim,
Everyday he gives us leftovers:
One a piece of bread,
The other a piece of horse,
And we are also done in deep.

Refrain: . . .

Verse 3:
The third Chaim of the house of life,
Made a good deal with the angel of death:
He should provide him more and more corpses;
He should provide them day and night.
So, the angel of death
Got to work right away.
He makes a mess out of every hero:
He does it quickly,
He does it well.
He makes the whole ghetto weak and tired.

Refrain: . . .

Verse 4:
On a summer day,
It was a very hot day,
Rumkowski walked in the street,
And looked like a Royal Highness.
He wore a light-colored suit, oy,
And dark glasses,
Surrounded by the police.
I tell you
Our Royal Highness has gray hair;
May he live to be a hundred!

Refrain: . . .

Verse 5:
Rumkowski Chaim, the Eldest of the Jews,
Is employed by the Gestapo.
We Jews are his brothers,

And he supplies our food.
He makes miracles, oy,
So every day,
For heaven's sake, oy, oy, oy!
Everyone asks:
A second question, oy?
Chaim says: It's good this way!

I have recorded an additional verse on Rumkowski, from Yaakov Flam, sung to the same melody. This verse was recalled and published by Frenkiel (1986b: 43–44), a survivor of the Lodz ghetto who considers it an independent song and not as a verse of this "hit song," even though it is sung to the same melody:

Verse 6:
Ikh hob aykh yidelekh epes tsi zugn:
A kadakhes vel ikh aykh zugn.
Di yidelekh zugn shoyn fil nevues,
"Az di geto efenen vet men shevues!"
A tsveytn tug er redt,
Yidelekh makhn shoyn a gevet
Un lernen zekh shoyn vayter trefn;
Rumkovski fin di yidelekh lakht:
"A krenk vus ir trakht!"
Di geto blaybt oykh vayter git farmakht.

Verse 6:
I've got for you, Jews, something to tell you:
It's a big nothing I've got to tell you.
The Jews mouth many prophecies already,
"The Ghetto will open
on Shavuot!"
A second day he makes a speech,
Jews are already betting
And trying to guess;
But Rumkowski laughs at the Jews:
"Who cares what you think!"
And still the ghetto stays tightly closed.

The song, especially the refrain, is known to every survivor of the Lodz ghetto. In addition, Yaakov Rotenberg even calls it *ha-shir ha-gadol* in Hebrew, meaning the "hit" song of the ghetto. Rachmil Bryks quotes the refrain in his novel *Der kayser in geto* (The emperor in the ghetto) and describes children and adults singing it, accompanying themselves with hand clapping and foot stamping

(1961:29). Bryks also quotes a variant of the refrain (1961:196) which was composed by the ghetto children for a play they performed on a street corner:

Rumkowski Chaim
Er get indz mayim,
Er get indz fefer,
Er get indz sam . . .
R'hot gemakht a gete mit a dyete.
R'hot gemakht a gete mit a mete—
Und er shrayt
Az er iz gerekht!

Rumkowski Chaim
He gives us water,*
He gives us pepper,
He gives us poison.
He made a ghetto
With a diet.
He made a ghetto
By the meter—
And he claims
That he is right!

Chava Rosenfarb in her trilogy *Der boym fun lebn* (The tree of life) also quotes an abridged version of the song (1972, 2:550).

The opening three verses speak in turn about the three "Chaims": Chaim Rumkowski; Chaim Weitzmann, the Zionist leader; and Chaim *der grober* (the fat), the undertaker of the ghetto. The latter's nickname is a multilevel pun relating to his physical appearance (*grober* in Yiddish means fat one) and to his profession (*gräber* is German for gravedigger). The real name of Chaim *der grober* was Chaim Perzerkowski; he survived the war and died soon after its end, in 1945 in Lodz.[5]

The final two verses give sarcastic praise to Rumkowski. These might be considered as dues paid to the "Royal Highness" so he would not get angry and arrest the singer. These verses could have been improvised when the singer saw Rumkowski in the streets, and were probably not composed at the same time as the first three verses. My sources could not give any dates for the composition in general or for any particular verses.

The sixth verse comments on Rumkowski's speechmaking, for while he favored big words in order to foster hope, his words actually contained nothing of substance.

Throughout the song, contrasts are made between "him," the leader, and "us," the ghetto dwellers. The name Chaim literally means "life," but the song which was composed in the ghetto has other important features. In its many-layered allusions to the heritage of Jewish cultural life, biblical themes, Hassidic folklore, and Zionism, "Rumkowski Chaim" is a powerfully ironic commentary on the abuses of power, the senseless infliction of suffering on one's fellow man, and the negation of life—death.

The following is my line-by-line interpretation of the text based on this background and the interviews I have conducted.

The word *khayim* (Yidd.: Chaim) serves as a leitmotif for the first verse as well as for the entire song. The song declares: "Jews are seen to be blessed with life, life until death." This statement has morbidly recast the biblical verse "For dust we thou art, and unto dust shall thou return" (Gen. 3:19), as "from the cemetery we are created and to the cemetery we return." (Cemetery = *beys ha-khayim,* that is, euphemistically, house of life.) An analogy is made between Chaim Rumkowski, the Jewish leader, and Moses, the Jewish historical leader. Chaim promised the ghetto dwellers miracles, promised them food (life) that would descend as a result of miracles, when in actuality the result of these promises is that they starved. However, when the ghetto dwellers complain, Rumkowski answers, "It's good this way." The question reflects their misery, but also Rumkowski's belief that he was doing the right thing.

The refrain makes clear the analogy to Moses: Moses gave his people the "manna" by miracles. Rumkowski, on the other hand, "gives us bran / he gives us barley / he gives us wine." The wine was made from barley, the informant explains, just as in the variant (quoted above) Rumkowski is like Moses and "gives us manna." But unlike the children of Israel in the desert, the ghetto-dwellers starve. Nothing is left but to complain. The wife complains to her husband, as described in the song: "Jews in the desert ate manna / Now each woman eats her husband." This plays on the Yiddish idiom *esn zikh*—to eat away at something; in this case the woman's complaints "eat up" her husband. The poet also plays on the rhyme-association—*manna,* the biblical sustenance, and *man,* Yiddish for husband. The poet gives an explanation as to how the ghetto reached its desperate condition, in the line "Rumkowski Chaim thought it through, / worked hard day and night, / made a ghetto with a diet." As Rute Pups (1962:56–58) explains, the word *dyeto* meant a special food store which carried better food products. Officially the store was for "sick people," but in fact it was for privileged people from whom Rumkowski wanted support. So, while Rumkowski and his friends are eating well, everyone else eats poorly.

The refrain reminded Hershkowitz's audience as to who was responsible for the deteriorating situation in the ghetto, describing the lack of resources and identifying the main cause of the suffering.

The repetition of the word *khayim* in the refrain brings to mind the blessing of the new month in which the reader and the congregation ask God for eleven different kinds of *khayim:* life. On the Sabbath preceding *Rosh Ḥodesh,* Jews call upon God: "grant us long life, a life of peace and well-being, a life of blessing and sustenance, a life of physical health, a life of piety and dread of sin, a life free from shame and disgrace, a life of wealth and honor, a life marked by our love for Torah and our fear of Heaven, a life in which the wishes of our heart shall be fulfilled for happiness" (translation in Birnbaum 1969 : 430). This contrast of a blessing which becomes a curse, life which is like death but not death itself, is the central motif of this song.

The second verse introduces Chaim Weizmann, the leader of the Zionist movement. Again the contrast is made: Chaim Weizmann entrapped the Jewish people in the Holy Land by telling them to work the soil; and in the ghetto, the dwellers work and yet receive *shirayim* (Heb.: leftovers). The reference to *shrayim* also requires some explanation: This Hebrew word for leftovers specifically refers to that part of the meal a Hassidic Rebbe would leave for his followers. In the song text this tributary food, originally an act of respect, is "a piece of bread, . . . a piece of horse" (the latter is not kosher). Yaakov Rotenberg recalls how Orthodox Jews spat at the singer when he mentioned the horsemeat. For many Jews, however, it was at that time the food that saved their lives. *Shrayim* rhymes with *khayim* (life), and *ferd* (horse, i.e., horsemeat = food = life) rhymes with *drerd* (the earth), making life like death.

The third verse presents the third Chaim, the gravedigger, who brings corpses to the "house of life," the cemetery. This Chaim, as described in the song, is very productive: "(He) made a good deal with the angel of death: / He should provide him more and more corpses; / He should provide them day and night." The "deal" was struck between the Angel of Death (the only angel known in the ghetto) and the undertaker. The Angel of Death is a good worker: he "got to work right away. / He makes a mess out of every hero. / He does it quickly, He does it well. / He makes the ghetto weak and tired." This efficient cooperation between the two creates a weak ghetto, or in some versions, a weak world—which for the inhabitants means probably the same thing. This partnership, made in heaven, causes dreadful results on earth.

Here the song could come to an end (as in Itka Slodowsky's version);[6] however Yaakov Rotenberg remembered two additional verses devoted exclusively to the "Royal Highness," the "First Chaim," Chaim Rumkowski.

The fourth verse begins with a description of a seasonal moment in the ghetto: it is a summer day, a hot summer day; Chaim Rumkowski wears a light-colored suit, his eyes are shielded by dark glasses. Why? Does he not wish to see what is going on in the ghetto? In his kingdom? In contrast to the cold and darkness suffered by the ghetto dwellers, a motif found in many songs of the period, the sun always shines for Rumkowski. He walks in the streets surrounded by personal guards; he is not alone "and look[s] like a Royal Highness." And the verse concludes: "I tell you / Our Royal Highness has gray hair; / May he live to be a hundred!" The poet tells his audience that although Rumkowski is not young—after all he was appointed to be the "Eldest of the Jews"—he wished him to live to be a hundred. This blessing is actually a curse, since Jews bless each other with *hundert und tsvontsik yor*—"may you live to be a hundred and twenty," the number of years that Moses lived (Deut. 34:7). Here, then, it becomes clear that Rumkowski is not Moses; as a "tribute" to his leadership even a hundred years are more than enough.

Yaakov Rotenberg and Rute Pups (1962:56–58) both report that when the singer used to sing the last line of that verse, "may he live to be a hundred," the audience would respond with an additional sarcastic sentence: *Az aynnemen zol er a shvarts yor,* meaning "May he live through a black year," i.e., may the devil take him. And thus they expressed their anger and "love" to their Royal Highness.

The fifth verse continues the line of thought presented in the fourth verse: yes, Rumkowski is the "Eldest of the Jews"; that is the title given to him by the Germans. He has to obey the *Gestapo,* but "We Jews are his brothers / and he supplies our food" (*papo* is the Polish word for cereal, meaning basic food). In addition one should not forget that "He makes miracles, so every day / for heaven's sake, oy, oy, oy."

The sixth verse is a commentary on Rumkowski's speeches, which created fear and at the same time hope. They were the source for rumors, and were delivered in a Lithuanian dialect; Rumkowski thought this to be the dialect of the Jewish intelligentia of which he wanted to become a part. Rumors such as "the ghetto will open on

Shavuot" were spread often, but this and other rumors were pure fantasy. *Shavuot* is the holiday that commemorates Moses' bringing the Torah (God's law) from Mount Sinai to the Children of Israel. However, in the ghetto there was no Torah, no Moses, no holiday, and no freedom; it remained tightly closed, its dwellers hopeless and weakened.

Dobroszycki writes, "Rumkowski rarely doubted that he was in the right" (1984:I). Indeed, Yankele Hershkowitz ends his song with the last words of its refrain manifesting the same idea.

The melody of "Rumkowski Chaim," which contributed to its popularity, may have been adapted from another source. The melody has many characteristics of Jewish folksong with reminders of cantorial recitation, and this may have been its origin. It is cast in a minor mode. It makes use of a distinctive rhythmic manner of text setting—iambic primas—a melodic-rhythmic figure with a universal repetition. This figure, according to Braun (1984:285 n. 44), is characteristic of Jewish folksong.

The song form is: verse, A A′ B B′; refrain, A A′ B B′. This form is common in both Jewish folk music (cf. Beregovski 1982:293) and European and Jewish popular music (cf. Idelsohn 1967:400). The verse and the refrain share similar rhythmic and melodic material. It is sung in a triple meter with an upbeat which causes asymmetric accents on weak beats. Like other Jewish folksongs, according to Beregovski (1982:293), the melody is symmetrical; the underlying structure of this song is in four measures.

The "sweet" melody with its ironic cantorial ornamentations carries a profound commentary on daily suffering in the ghetto. The match between the text and the melody caused the song to live in the memory of the survivors.

NOTES

1. For a fictionalized account of this most interesting character of World War II, see Leslie Epstein, *King of the Jews* (New York: Avon Books, 1979).

2. Dawidowicz compares Rumkowski with Moses Merin of Sosnowiec, another leader who was flattered by the power given to him and who used it (1975:226–27).

3. Possibly the "new song" mentioned by the ghetto chronicle refers to a song which is a parody on a Yiddish folksong, "Lebn zol Bistrizky und zein hora" (Long live Bistrizky and his horah), or "Lebn zol undzer khaver Stalin (Long live our friend Stalin), a prewar folksong which none of the informants could recall. In his article (1985:65), Yaakov Gelman transcribes one verse of this song, which is based on the recording made by the Historical

Committee in Munich in 1946, and which is available at Yad-Vashem and at the Sound Archive of the National Library in Jerusalem. In the same article he discusses another song about the "two Chaims," the undertaker and Chaim Rumkowski (1985:69–71) based on the same recordings. In that song the two Chaims agree to divide the world's government: one will be in charge of death and the other in charge of life. This song, as with most of the songs of the Historical Committee, is unknown to the informants I interviewed, and therefore is not included in the text.

4. In this version, recorded from Yaakov Rotenberg, there are three words which he sings differently each time: he sings *vayn* (wine) instead of "man." However, he said that the correct version is "man" (*manna*), but changed it as he remembered that they made wine from barley. He sings "yeyder giber" (every hero) in one recording, and in another he sings "yeyder ayner" (everyone). He also sings in one place "geto" (ghetto) and then "velt" (world) in the fourth verse. He also omits or shortens the beginning of the refrain, indicated by the brackets. These variations are evidence that the songs are still alive in his mind.

Like the word *dyeto* explained in the text, the word *mayim* (literally, water) in the ghetto slang became the proper name for another entity, ghetto soup.

5. Chaim Perzerkowski's son survived and carried on the family tradition in Israel, where he served as the supervisor of a hospital morgue. I interviewed him in May 1990 about his and his father's experiences in the ghetto.

6. Interview with Itka Slodowsky, Bat-Yam, 10 September 1985.

3

Yaakov and the Street Songs

"Rumkowski Chaim" was the hit song of the street song genre. Other street songs, if not so prominent in the memory of Holocaust survivors, nevertheless reveal a great deal about the history of the ghetto and about those who sang them. Yaakov Rotenberg sang most of the street songs presented in this chapter; it is instructive to look first at his life story.

Yaakov's Story

Yaakov Rotenberg was born in Lodz in 1926. He was forced to move with his parents, his three younger sisters, and his elderly grandmother into the ghetto, where he was interned until 1944. He was later transported to Auschwitz and from there to a labor camp in Gleiwitz, where he was liberated by the Russians. The only member of his family to survive, he immigrated to Israel in 1948. He now lives in Givatayim, with his wife and two children.

It was Yaakov, in fact, who conducted the interview. He had prepared himself for my visit and rehearsed in his mind the main themes for our discussion. He did not enjoy being interrupted by my questions and insisted on telling me when to turn on my tape recorder and when to shut it off. Unlike Miriam Harel, Yaakov did not want to tell me about his life; rather, he wished to discuss four themes which he defined as fear, the cruelty of the Germans, sacrifice, and heroism. These themes were to be the core of the interview. Although he was aware that the songs he remembered were my primary interest, he had prepared a selection on cassette before I arrived. Throughout the interview he sang several fragments of the songs to illustrate certain points.

Yaakov was worried that I would not be able to withstand the emotion of his story. He asked me to tell him when I felt it was becoming "too hard for me." He told me that he was no longer concerned about himself; his wife, however, worried about him and she was present throughout the interview session.

Yaakov organized his experiences around the four themes listed above; that was how he chose to relate them to me and it is thus that I will present them.[1]

Fear

> We were educated to be afraid. When you see a drunk Gentile staggering on one side of the street, cross over to the other side. When you see a fight, go away. I was educated this way. I was educated to be afraid. When the Germans came in, they persecuted the Jews drastically. They kidnapped Jews for work. How did they do it? Two armed Germans stood in the street. A Jew was walking by. One German put a gun against his head, and the other one asked him to come with him. The Jew had no choice. He came. Then, they gathered a group of Jews, took them to work, and brought them back in the evening. In the evening was a curfew. Jews could not walk in the streets, Jews could not get food. This was even before the ghetto. To get bread, one had to stand in line. So we stood in line, and they took us out of the line. How did the Germans and the Poles know that we are Jews? Because of our behavior: because of our fear.

Yaakov felt that it was very important for me to understand fear. He assumed that as a native Israeli I had never experienced it, and in order for me to grasp fully the events of those times, I ought to try to identify with the people living through them.

Cruelty

> The Germans took ten Jews and sat them in a row on a bench. They ordered the first one to come in. He walked in and all the other nine heard a terrible screaming. After a couple of minutes, a German dressed in a bloodstained white robe, holding a butcher's knife full of blood, came out of the room and told the second Jew to come in. The other eight were still waiting. The second one went in. All the rest heard his screaming and the German came out with the same knife covered with fresh blood. The people waiting were faint with fear, trembling, until their own time arrived. Among them was my father. By the time he was called, he was almost frightened to death. He simply thought that the German was going to kill him. But when he walked in, he saw the Jews sitting in a row on a bench, plucking duck's feathers. When each was called in, the German slaughtered a duck, and commanded the Jew to scream and pluck off the duck's feathers. Can you understand the cruelty of this kind of mind?

Sacrifice

Yaakov began another story in order to explain to me about sacrifice. He then immediately instructed me to turn off my tape recorder. When I had permission again to turn it on, the story was at its end. While the machine was running, Yaakov spoke of other issues. After the interview was over, I thanked him and he said: "Why do you thank me, do you want to go? I still have not told you about sacrifice." Then he told me two stories, the first of which begins thus:

> There was a rabbi from Germany who was brought to the ghetto. He was translating the Talmud from Hebrew to German for the Germans. He was probably a great scholar. I met him in 1943. He used to gather a *minyan* for Yom Kippur and my mother and I both joined. At that time I was still saying *kaddish* for my later father. After the *minyan* he gave a *drasha*—a speech in which he attacked the Germans. He was very loyal to the Jewish nation. It was not a provocative speech—it was his belief. This was my first meeting with him.

He continued the narrative so as to reach the real sacrifice:

> I met him for the second time after we passed the gates of Auschwitz, after we passed the "shower." The ones who survived the shower, survived. And there I saw him, surrounded by a small group of Jews preaching again. He preached to them—and I tell you about him so this dear Jew will not be forgotten. He arrived in Auschwitz with his beautiful daughter and his grandson. The Germans wanted to take his daughter to the house of ill fame. They gave the child to another woman. The rabbi was not afraid; he understood what the Germans were about to do. He gathered his daughter and grandson and brought them to the section of the camp where people were sent to die, and both were burned. In his speech there he said: "It is better that I sacrifice my daughter than let her be a prostitute for the Germans."

And Yaakov repeated, "This story should not be forgotten. This Jew did not survive. I inquired and found out that he died in a labor camp in Jaworzno. Things like that happened to the Jewish people. These things are so significant in the Jewish mind. I do not know if I expressed it well enough, I do not know if you in your work will be able to transmit the depth of that. This was one of the manifestations of this sacrifice I am talking about."

Sacrifice is a prominent theme in Jewish life. The sacrifice of the beloved son by his father is well known from the story of Abraham and Isaac. But the question of where God was remains unanswered.

Yaakov received a Jewish education before the war. Later, in the ghetto, he was a member of the Zionist organization Gordonya for a short time. In Israel he lived as a secular Jew, like most of the survivors who grew up in this youth organization. Several years ago, however, after his daughter converted to orthodoxy, he changed his life drastically and became a religious Jew, living according to the principles of Jewish law. It may be that the "theme" (as he calls it) of sacrifice became more significant to him as he delved into his own religion. He spoke about sacrifice in a special way that was almost biblical, full of piety and respect.

He continued with a second narrative, "maybe parallel to the previous one, but of another character," to demonstrate the nature of sacrifice. This story took place in a labor camp:

> We were several men from Lodz in one camp, called Gleiwitz Four. One day we came back from work and we were all searched. The Germans were looking for an electric wire. Someone pulled out the electric wire from the bathroom with the lamp. The Germans wanted to know who took the wire and why. One thought that someone had stolen it to hold up his trousers which were too large. So, therefore we all were searched. But they could not find the wire. So the Germans explained that as a punishment we would be forced to do sit-ups for hours after work—an awful punishment. So one of the Jews volunteered to say, "I did it. Instead of the torture of all of us, I will go." And he was about to. He was in the third row back, and the Jews in the second row stopped him. One said, "If you went without explaining, we would have let you go, but since you said you are going in order to save us, we will not let you go. What will be with us will be with you." So he stayed and we were all punished. We did the sit-ups and when we became exhausted the Germans took the lash to us. It was terrible. Then someone said in Yiddish, "We shall overcome it." And after him everyone repeated, "We shall all overcome it." This went on for several days. We worked, and then were punished. Then, one day one of the other Germans found out what was going on with us. He said, "These Jews did not pull the electric wire, I did. The enemy was bombing from the air, and I did not want our camp observed, so I removed the power wire. I forgot to report it when I went on vacation." The German did not report and we were punished.

This is the story, but Yaakov explains the point: "The point is not the punishment and not the event, but the spirit of the individual who could make the sacrifice. And the spirit of the others who did not want to sacrifice him in order to survive. This is even a greater sacrifice. To receive a sacrifice is even easier than to do it. To make a sacrifice, to refuse a sacrifice, this is the important point I wanted to tell you about."

In this story sacrifice is associated with heroism, the two central themes Yaakov wants to remember and transmit.

Heroism

Yaakov Rotenberg mentions heroism as manifested in a street singer whose name he does not recall. A short Jew who went from street corner to street corner singing revolutionary songs, the man would stand on a stool, raise his right fist, and sing out, "One must fight." Yaakov explained, "The song is not important. The important thing is the expression in the hand movement." (Cf. song 5.)

The call for revolt in the ghetto, the actions people took in public, are for Yaakov heroic acts. The songs he recalls are a representation of the common destiny of the Jews. Yaakov does not talk about himself and his life. He talks about "us," the Jews, and "them," the Germans, the Poles, and other groups. He recalls songs which were in the public domain, such as street songs and theater songs.

He explains that he remembered his repertoire of street and theater songs because he was a young boy at the time:

> I was wandering around the ghetto. At the beginning of the ghetto I did not work and fortunately enough I did not go to school. When I came to register for school I saw a big line and I said I would come tomorrow. All the children who registered went with the first transports to their death. The next day, they did not open the registration. So I was without a job, without school, and without friends and people to keep me company. A human being always strives for something. So I found the songs. A song is also something. It is a relaxing drug for people. It was something like that for me. At that time I did not understand the significance of these songs. Now I do; when one listens to a song he escapes from everyday life, he escapes from his despair.

This is Yaakov's personal psychological explanation. His other explanation is both textual and contextual: "These songs reflected the everyday reality. They served in place of newspapers, radios, and other forms of entertainment." A song had to be based on everyday life to attract attention, because singers live on the mercy and pockets of their audience.

When the ghetto was sealed, Yaakov's father went to work as a janitor for his portion of bread. After his father died, Yaakov's mother requested the job, which she obtained. Yaakov, seeing her difficulties, asked to be transferred from his job in the coal storage department to this department of ghetto maintenance. Thus he worked for himself, for his mother, and also for others cleaning houses and streets.

One of the people he helped was a theater makeup artist. As a result of their relationship, this man would take him to the theater. He used to carry his makeup case and would enter the theater from backstage. "The theater was a different world. A world of actors and actresses, all singing, humming, constant motion. And I was in the middle of this action. So I saw some theater shows."

Yaakov was attracted to people from whom he could learn something. That is how he became friends with Yelin, the makeup artist, and with Rachmil Bryks, the writer. The latter, lonely and suffering from the cold, used to sit in the area Yaakov had to clean. So Yaakov would bring him some hot water, and make him a special kind of ghetto coffee. From Bryks, Yaakov learned about writing.

As a natural-born leader, Yaakov felt the need to speak in defense of Rumkowski. He thought that Rumkowski organized the ghetto in a very efficient way and honestly tried to help the Jews of Lodz. He attempted to be fair. Unfortunately, it took the Russians four to five extra months to reach Lodz (because of difficulties in liberating Warsaw), a delay which allowed the Germans to deport sixty to seventy thousand Jews to the death camps. If the Russians had arrived earlier, these Jews could have been saved and Rumkowski would have been their savior. Yaakov concludes, "One should not judge him in a superficial way, not judge him quickly without knowing the facts."

He also told me that there were two other groups of people whom we must remember: the German Jews, and the Gypsies.

The German Jews could not adjust to the ghetto conditions and almost all of them perished. Yaakov describes their tragedy with pain: "I have no words to tell you how they disappeared. They came from a completely different life. Their dignity and self-esteem were so low when they arrived. They found themselves humiliated and unable to adjust psychologically, not like the Polish Jews who were used to bad conditions all the time in Poland. As a young boy, watching these people suffer left a strong pain in me, I can't even talk about it; I've never talked about it before." Yet, this trauma reminded him of a song describing the tragedy of the *Yekes* (Yiddish name for German Jews): "S'geyt a yeke" (It's a Yeke walks around) (see song 14).

The other group is the Gypsies, who had a special quarter in the ghetto: "They were completely isolated, and they were killed very fast. They were killed like dogs. Many musical instruments were found among their belongings when taken away. They were very intelligent, maybe they were diplomats? During some months they deported every single one, and there was no memory of this horror."[2]

Yaakov's life story is not complete. However, this trauma, expressed in his testimony and the songs he remembered and collected, helps us to understand the repertoire of songs in the Lodz ghetto. At the present time Yaakov has turned to writing poems of his own in Hebrew.

The Street Songs

Yaakov Rotenberg's interpretation provides the key to the reconstruction of the original context of his songs. In each one, the text, transcribed into Latin characters, follows the pronunciation of the informants in their special Lodz dialect, as in the "hit song" discussed earlier.[3] Yaakov always sings the refrain before the verse and that is how I introduce the songs.

The title of each song is taken from the first line that the subject sings (which is the first line of the refrain, as in "Rumkowski Chaim"). When Yaakov supplies an additional title to a song, I include it in brackets under the first title.

In addition, I append verses and songs from other sources. An English translation is given for the transcription of the text. The translation does not imitate the rhyme scheme of the poetry, but follows closely the meaning of the text.

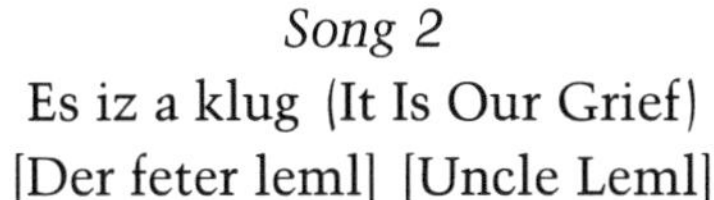

Song 2
Es iz a klug (It Is Our Grief)
[Der feter leml] [Uncle Leml]

Refren:
Es iz a klug,
Es iz tsi indz a tsure!
Es iz a klug,
Es helft nisht kayn geshray!
Nor mier lodzer,
Zenen di kapure!
Es iz azayn gebot:
Der kligster blaybt haynt a idiot.

Verse:
Ikh hob a feter hayst er leml,
Er iz kerovnik bay di *straż*.
Er rirt zikh pinkt zo vi a keml;
A fayer lesht er mit a flash.

Refren:
Es iz a klug . . .

Refrain:
It is our grief,
It is our problem!
It is our grief,
It won't help to complain!
But we Lodzers
Are being sacrificed!
It is a sort of commandment:
The wise man stays an idiot.

Verse:
I have an uncle, his name is Leml,
He is the head of the Fire Department.
He moves as swiftly as a camel;
He puts out fires with a bottle.

Refrain:
It is our grief . . .

The song is a commentary on the "protection pill" system of Rumkowski (favoritism), who appointed his favorites for the preferred positions held in the ghetto. In doing that, of course, he did not consider the relevant qualifications but rather the relationship according to his "understanding."

This song was sung toward the end of 1940 and was remembered by many survivors because of its satirical but realistic description of "Uncle Leml." "Uncle Leml" rhymes in another version with "Kuni Leml," one of the stock characters from the Yiddish theater, from the play *Kuni Leml* (1870) by Goldfadn.

Frenkiel (1986b:48) includes a second verse which presents the same idea with another example of the system of "favoritism":

A komisar ken ikh zayer a kliger.
Ikh gay mit aykh a gevet:
Az onfirn ken er nor mit flign,
Dertsu iz er an analfabet.

I know a clever Komisar.
I'll make with you a bet:
That only flies would follow him,
Besides which he's illiterate.

Following the publication of his article (1986b), Frenkiel claimed in a meeting with me that this song was not composed by Yankele Hershkowitz but by the theater writer Shimeon Janowski. It may have been that the song was first introduced in the theater and was later sung in the streets, a common "way" for popular tunes.

The melody, in a minor key, reminds the listener of the internationally popular tango due to its rhythmic pattern in which all beats are sharply accented and occasionally interrupted by sudden pauses or emphatically syncopated passages. The tango remained popular throughout the twentieth century, and its popularity was probably the reason for its use in this context.

Song 3

Geto, getunya (Ghetto, Oh Little Ghetto)

Refren:
Geto, getunya, getokhna, kokhana,
Tish taka malutka e taka shubrana,
Der vos hot a hant a shtarke,
Der vos hot oyf zikh a marke,
Krigt fin shenstn in fin bestn,
Afile a postn oykh dem grestn.
Ven di bist inteligent,

On a sent,
Drayste dikh arim vi a mes.
On a broyt in un adres,
In di zingst oyf terkish zikh,
Oy es (yes).

Verse 1:
Meydlakh zikh ale shemen,
Nisht kayn shminke nisht kayn bremen,
Nisht kayn tabarin nisht kayn fayf,
Nisht ruz kayn andulatsie,
Nisht kayn miteg, kayn kulatsie,
Zay hobn tsi vashn nisht kayn zayf.
Nor pzimartovyene zayt nisht tsitsi pulkes.
In ale zingt mit meye dem refrayn:
Oy, oy, oy.

Refren: Geto, getunya . . .

Verse 2:
Nisht zorgn in nisht kleyrn,
S'vet bay indz git nokh veyrn,
S'vet dekh kartofl oykh du zayn.
Men iz shoyn korev meykakh,
Yom tov vet men esn leykekh,
Trinkn fin gropn karmel vayn,
Nor pzimartovyene zayt nisht tsitsi pulkes.
In ale zingt mit meye dem refrayn:
Oy, oy, oy.

Refren: Geto, getunya . . .

Refrain:
Ghetto, oh little ghetto, oh ghetto my love,
You are so small and so poor,
Everyone who has a strong hand,
Everyone who wears the mark,
Gets the best of everything,
He also gets a job—the best.
However, if you are intelligent,
Without a cent,
You will walk around like the dead.
With no bread and no address,
And you will sing to yourself in Turkish,
Oy, eat! (Oh yes).

Verse 1:
The girls are all ashamed,
They've got no makeup, got no eyeliner,
No bed, no whistling,

No rouge, no permanent-wave hair,
No lunch, no dinner,
They have not got soap to wash themselves.
Just do not be cheap women.
So everyone sing with me the refrain:
Oy, oy, oy

Refrain: Ghetto, oh little ghetto . . .

Verse 2:
Do not worry and don't fret,
Someday things will be good for us here,
We will soon eat potatoes here.
The time will come, soon,
We will eat cake on holidays,
We will drink Carmel wine,
Just do not be cheap women.
So everyone sing with me the refrain:
Oy, oy, oy

Refrain: Ghetto, oh little ghetto . . .

This song, composed and sung by Yankele Hershkowitz, is a commentary on events that took place in the ghetto during late summer 1940.[4] The burdens of distress and lack of work caused the ghetto inhabitants to protest against Rumkowski, and they held demonstrations. Rumkowski, whose life was threatened, decided to establish a Jewish police for personal protection, the *Sonderkommando,* which was detailed for internal affairs. To this special police section he appointed all the physically strong men he could find in the ghetto.

Full of irony, the song begins with the refrain as a love song for a woman. The small, weak woman, however, symbolizes the ghetto inhabitants, while the strong men are the *Sonderkommando;* they are there not really to keep the women alive but to keep themselves alive, strong, and happy. The strong man gets "the best of everything, he also gets a job—the best," while the "poor, intelligent" man "walks around like the dead."

And what is left for the inhabitants? Singing. In every language they are singing that they want to eat. In one version I recorded, the informant (Itka Slodowsky) substituted "Oy yes" for "Oy es."[5] Noting the bilingual pun, she explained that it was proof the audience was sophisticated and expected to comprehend such wordplay.

In this song the whole situation is described in negative terms. The verse uses a number of ghetto slang words, such as *kolacja* (Yidd.: *kulatsie*), a Polish word for "dinner"; in this context it refers to a meal given as a prize to the good workers once in fourteen days at the public kitchens (Dobroszycki 1984: 510).

The second verse has a different ending in Frenkiel (1986b: 47) and in *Min Hametsar* (Blumental 1951: 132–33), which was probably forgotten by Rotenberg and even Slodowsky; they therefore repeat the same ending as the first verse. I should mention that Rotenberg and Slodowsky met to "complete" the fragments for each other.

Frenkiel's versions are very helpful in explaining some of the text's "illogical" content. In Frenkiel's essay and in *Min Hametsar*, the last two lines of the verse bring back the "favoritism" idea of Rumkowski's specially appointed henchmen:

> Der vos hot vet esn dubeltove,
> Un der vos nisht—
> Vet grizsen a bayn.
>
> The one who has will eat double portions,
> And the one who has not—
> Will chew on a bone.

The beginning of the verse sounds optimistic. To paraphrase, "we will soon eat potatoes, . . . cakes, . . . we shall drink Carmel wine." For the singer, however, these are only past memories and hopes for the future, while for Rumkowski's favorites these benefits constitute the present.

Min Hametsar (Blumental 1951: 132–33) has a third verse to the song, in which the inhabitants are called upon to produce new babies so they can get more money to buy the food rations. The underlying implication is, of course, that it is foolhardy to do that.

The melody of this song is probably of Jewish origin. It is reminiscent of a Jewish cumulative song such as "A Geneyve" (Rubin 1985: 10). Humorous songs of this type are common in Yiddish folk tradition. "A Geneyve" and "Geto getunya's" verses are based on short melodic motives in sequences to which one could add ever-increasing numbers of sequences according to the lyrics.

Song 4

S'iz kaydankes kaytn (It's Shackles and Chains)

Refren:
S'iz kaydankes kaytn,
S'iz gite tsaytn,
Kayner tit zikh haynt nisht shemen,
Yeder vil du haynt nor nemen;
Abi tsi zayn du zat.

Verse 1:
Nekhtn a levaye,
Geveyzn a geshray,
Mit agole genovim,
Zikh gegebn a gite dray.
Mentshn fil mit shrek,
Dray meysim vern geyl.
S'iz kayn meysim gur geveyzn,
Nor dray zek mit meyl.

Refren:
S'iz kaydankes kaytn . . .

Verse 2:
S'ganvet moyshe, s'ganvet khayim,
S'ganvet oyekh nisl.

Mit yadayim nemt men shrayim
Fin di kohel's shisl.
Afile pesl fin'm kesl,
Nemt oyekh arup.
Yedn tug gist men vaser,
Dus iz indzer zup.

Refren:
S'iz kaydankes kaytn . . .

Verse 3:
[Rumkovski speaks:]
Hit aykh fil genovim,
Ikh vel aykh arestirn!
Ikh vel di gantse geto
Oyf aygene hent firn.
In oykh a priv koperativ:
Ale zenen blat!
S'iz fil meysim, fil taneysim,
Ver iz haynt du zat?

Refren:
S'iz kaydankes kaytn . . .

Refrain:
It's shackles and chains,
It's good times again,
No one feels shame,
Everyone only wants to grab;
Just so his stomach will be full.

Verse 1:
Yesterday, a funeral,
There was an outcry,
A cart with thieves,
Turned upside down.
People were aghast,
Three "corpses" turning yellow.
But not corpses after all,
Just three sacks of flour.

Refrain:
It's shackles and chains . . .

Verse 2:
Moishe steals, Chaim steals,
Nissl steals as well.
With their hands they grab leftovers
From the community pot.
Even Pessl from the kettle
Grabs whatever's in there.

Every day they add some water,
This is our soup.

Refrain:
It's shackles and chains . . .

Verse 3:
[Rumkowski speaks:]
Be on guard, all you thieves,
I'll arrest you!
I want the entire ghetto
Under our firm, strong hand.
By decree of the Cooperative:
All of you are guilty!
There are corpses, there is mourning,
Who is full today?

Refrain:
It's shackles and chains . . .

"Kaydankes kaytn" was composed by Yankele Hershkowitz as a commentary on the thievery common in the ghetto, and on one event in particular: the theft of three sacks of flour in the guise of a funeral. The versions of the song as remembered by Yaakov Rotenberg and Itka Slodowsky are nearly identical; Yaakov Flam's rendition, however, differed in the number and order of lines. The song dates from the early days of the ghetto, probably during the fall or winter of 1940. It is also included in the 1946 recordings of the Historical Committee of Munich, which are deposited in the National Sound Archives in Jerusalem. The recordings do not include any commentary or documentation.

The refrain describes the "good times" which came to the ghetto. Once more the poet uses the idea of "good" to mean "bad"—in this case, shortages of food, and low moral standards.

The second verse supplies the details of the general phenomenon described in the refrain: Who steals? Everyone. Ordinary people like Moishe, Chaim, Nissl, and even Pessl, the one who ladles the soup. What do they steal? *Shrayim* (leftovers). Here the text clearly parallels that of the popular ghetto song "Rumkowski Chaim," but with "Rumkowski Chaim" the special leftovers become ordinary poor leftovers.

Theft, especially of food, was an everyday occurrence in the ghetto. The *Chronicle* reports many instances of thievery in the ghetto and expresses sympathy with the starving population at the same time. In the entry of 19 December 1943, for example, Oskar Rosenfeld writes: ". . . on a single day, six cases of theft were reported by the Special Unit. Six cases, but at bottom, one motive: hunger! . . . So it goes at the Sonderkommando (Special Unit). The Court is more severe, more faithful to the letter of the law. But life in the ghetto has no respect for either the police or the court. It makes its own laws, even if they lead to arrest or excrement-removal duty" (Dobroszycki 1984:418-19).

According to Yaakov Rotenberg, Rumkowski speaks to the Jews in the third verse of "Kaydankes Kaytn," in his Lithuanian dialect. In this speech he warns his Jews that he will arrest anyone caught stealing, and speaks also about the need for a strong, independent ruler in the ghetto. Frenkiel (1986b:49) includes an additional verse unknown to my informants. Also, he sang for me a variant of the opening two verses:

Alts ganvet genayve,
Ikh tu es azoy gut firn:
Koym khap ikh vemen
Baym minstn shvindl,
Bald vel ikh ihm arestirn.

Everywhere are thieves and thievery,
But I manage the place so well:
That when I catch anyone
In mid-swindle,
Right away, I arrest him.

And he continues with a verse in which Rumkowski speaks to his people, stating his policy and boasting of his activities on behalf of the weak and poor people:

Ikh vel aykh lernen seykhl,
Oyb ikh vet nisht folgn,
On a brekl rakhmones.
Gemakht a kolonie far kinder,
Und oykh far zkeynim,
Itst makh ikh oykh far almones.

I will teach you morals,
And if you don't obey them,
I will show no mercy.
I have set up a pension for children,
And for the aged folk,
And soon I'll set up one for widows, too.

My sources attributed this song to street singer Yankele Hershkowitz. However, Frenkiel claims that the story of the "flour corpses" (verses 1, 2, 3) was included in the first Revue Show of the "Vegetable Ressorts"; he includes the song under the title "Dray zek meyl" (Three sacks of flour). *Min Hametsar* (Blumental 1951 : 142) also refers to the song by this title. This number was popular in the ghetto, leading the head of the *Sonderkommando* to remove it from the show.

The melody of this song has a strong Jewish character. Khane Mlotek, a prominent researcher of Yiddish folksongs at the YIVO archives, notes that its beginning comes from another Yiddish song, titled "Vu nemt men parnose" (Where can one make a living?).[6]

The song is in the *frigish* mode, a minor mode with augmented second used in Jewish music; the mode became a musical symbol for popular Yiddish music in America (Slobin 1982 : 182–97). Though it is not exclusively characteristic of Jewish music, this mode does play an important role in Jewish folk and popular music. Ghetto songs, however, make infrequent use of the *frigish* mode. Unlike in the New World, ethnic identity was obviously not an issue in the ghetto.[7]

The following selection (songs 5, 6, 7) is a medley that begins and ends with the refrain of "Kemfn" (Fight). For Yaakov Rotenberg "Kemfn" was the most effective call for revolt in the ghetto, and perhaps this is why he sings it twice. Also, the first and the third songs in the medley call for a fight, and were therefore included. The second song was included because its melody is similar to the verse of the first song. The songs in the order given by Rotenberg are as follows:

Song 5: "Kemfn—Merin Der Nayer Kayser—Kemfn" (Fight—Merin the New Emperor—Fight)
Song 6: "Ikh hob gemakht kokletn" (I've made meatballs)
Song 7: "Yidishe politsay" (Jewish police)
Repeat of Song 5: "Kemfn" (Fight).

Song 5

Men darf tsi kemfn (One Must Fight)

[Kemfn / Merin Der Nayer Kayser] [Fight / Merin the New Emperor]

Refren:
Men darf tsi kemfn,
Shtark tsi kemfn,
Oy az der arbayter zol nisht laydn noyt!
Men tur nisht shvagn,
Nor hakn shabn;
Oy vet er ersht gringer krign a shtikl broyt.

Verse:
Merin der nayer keyser,
Er iz a yid a heyser,
Er shtamt fin klaynem shtetl,
Er hot amul gehat a berdl.
Er zugt indz tsi tsi geybn,
Men zol es nor darleybn,
Poylen bay dem yeke
Men zol efenen di geto.

Refren:
Men darf tsi kemfn . . .

Refrain:
One must fight,
Fight strong,
So that the worker will not suffer need!
One cannot be quiet,
But has to break windows;
That makes it easier to get a piece of bread.

Verse:
Merin, the new emperor,
He is a hot Jew,
He comes from a small shtetl,
He used to have a beard.
He promised us
That we should live to see the day,
When he makes the Germans
Open up the ghetto.

Refrain:
One must fight . . .

Yaakov Rotenberg commented, "The most important song in the ghetto was a song of revolt, 'Kemfn,' which means to fight." Rotenberg sang the refrain twice during the interview, stating that the song was a "call for fight and vengeance."

Did he feel that way in the ghetto, or is that only his later interpretation? In my opinion the word *kemfn* aroused other connotations forty years after the liberation. The song was a call for a demonstration of the workers, not a general call to fight for freedom.

The refrain calls for "the fight," the challenge for workers' rights so that they might earn enough money for food. This is definitely a call for survival, for social rights and revolt. The idea of "breaking windows" instead of keeping quiet was dominant at the beginning of the ghetto; however, the more organized the ghetto became, the more humiliated and weak the inhabitants, the more muted was the call to fight. (The refrain, which is included in Rute Pups's version of "The Demonstration," is repeated there three times [1962:62–63].)

The verse is a political satire on the rumor that the ghetto will get a new ruler known for his good qualities, one who may ask the Germans to open the ghetto. Moses Merin, a member of the central committee of the Eldest of the Jews in East-Upper Silesia in Sosnowiec, visited Lodz in the fall of 1940. Because he had a good reputation, there was hope that he might be the one to help the Lodz inhabitants. But, in fact, as mentioned above (chap. 2, n. 2), he resembled Rumkowski in his abuse of power. (In the version of the song published in Pups's book, this verse is the final one of the song.)

The melody comes from an earlier song by David Beyglman, "Ganovim lid—Masmatn" (Thieves' song). It is altered according to the new text, especially at the beginning of the verse and the beginning of the refrain, where the poet-singer adds some words and notes to adjust his new creation to the melody.

The same melody is used for song 10, below, "Amerike hot erklert." The original melody of "Ganovim lid—Masmatn" is at the YIVO archives and was published in the *Forward,* one of the few remaining Yiddish newspapers, by Khane and Yosl Mlotek in November 1989.

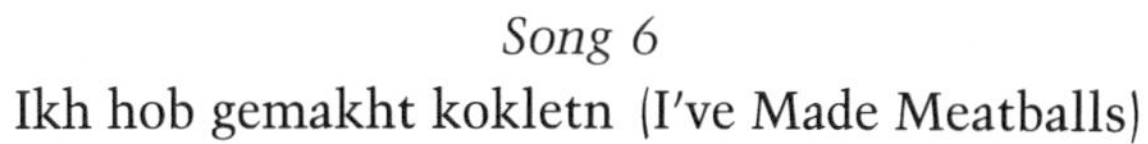

Song 6

Ikh hob gemakht kokletn (I've Made Meatballs)

Ikh hob gemakht kokletn,
Tsilib ale yidn.
In fin ferder's flaysh kokletn,
Zenen mentshn oykh tsefridn.
Men shtelt avek oyf shpeyter shtayn,
Vet es bald farshtinken,
Trinkt men nokh a gleyzl tay,
Mit a sakharinke.
Bim bom bim bom biribom,
Bim bim bom biribiribom.

I've made meatballs,
For all the Jews.
And from horse's flesh, meatballs,
The people are satisfied.
When this meat stands a while,
It starts to stink,
We drink a glass of tea,
With a little saccharine.
Bim bom bim bom biribom,
Bim bim bom biribiribom.

To a melody similar to that of the verse on Merin, Yaakov sings a fragment of a song about the most controversial food served in the ghetto: horsemeat. The desirability of eating horsemeat, though it was not kosher, must be reconsidered when hunger and starvation loom. According to Freda Burns (b. 1929, Lodz),[8] most of the ghetto accepted rabbinical dispensation and consumed the horseflesh; the orthodox, however, would not eat this ghetto delicacy.

This controversy does not arise in the song; however, the fact that horsemeat is used as a subject hints at its exoticism and its availability at the time. The description of the food is realistic: the meat is not the best and spoils very quickly, but when there is nothing else to eat, people are happy with meatballs made of horsemeat. To get rid of the taste people might drink a glass of tea sweetened with saccharine.

This verse also forms part of a different song entitled "Ferd-flaysh" (Horsemeat) (Pups 1962:37–39), in which hunger is described in a tragically realistic way: mothers are going in vain to look for food for their children, and they envy the dead. They would eat anything, even horsemeat. Pups dates the song to the early days of the ghetto, circa 1940, when the initial hunger was accompanied by panic.

Song 7

Gefloygn iz ales (Everything Is Up in the Air)

[Yidishe politsay] [Jewish Police]

Refren:
Gefloygn iz ales in di lift arayn,
Tsibl, mayrn, burkes, vorshtn, khrayn.
Gekimen zene yidishe politsay,
A kamf tsizamen shtoys,
Pinkt vi in ershtn may.

Verse:
Mir veln kemfn,
Oyf leybn in oyf toyt,
Biz ir velt nisht geybn
A tele zup mit broyt.
Biz ir velt nisht geybn
Burkes mit salat,
Dus leybn tsi derhaltn,
In tsi zayn nor zat.

Refren:
Gefloygn iz ales . . .

Refrain:
Everything is up in the air,
Onions, carrots, beets, salami, horseradish.
Get the Jewish police to come,
To combat the crowd,
Just like on the First of May.

Verse:
We shall fight,
In life and death,

Chaim Rumkowski after a demonstration. Zonabend Collection, YIVO Institute for Jewish Research.

Until you give us
A bowl of soup and bread.
Until you give us
Beets and salad,
To keep us alive,
And to be full.

Refrain:
Everything is . . .

This song concerns a demonstration that took place in the ghetto in early 1940; it was quelled by the Jewish police together with a special arm of the German militia. The demonstration ended when the Germans fired on the crowd (see Dobroszycki 1984: 5 n. 5).

Both the refrain and the single verse mention food. Here, however, food is used as a weapon of protest. As precious as food was, the ghetto inhabitants hurled it back at the Jewish police, venting their rage with the same weapon used against them. The verse is a powerful call to arms: "We shall fight in life and death," we shall fight for food "to keep us alive."

The melody of this song has its origins probably in a popular marching tune; it is in a major key and uses a march rhythm. A recapitulation of "Kemfn" concludes Yaakov Rotenberg's medley.

Song 8

In geto s'iz du a shteyger (The Notorious Ghetto) [Czarnieckego Znany] [The Notorious Czarnieckego]

In geto s'iz du a shteyger,
Es klapt shoyn vi a zeyger,
Alts iz du markotno,
Nishtu kayn *bez-rebotno.*
Men est gebrutns,
Men shpilt in kurtn,
Der gantser bayrat iz haynt mat.
Er hot kayn breyre,
Far an'veyre,
Der prezes shtarker iz a khvat.

The notorious ghetto,
It runs like clockwork,
Everything is in order,
No unemployment.
They eat roast,
Play cards,
The entire *Beirat* is corrupt.
He [Rumkowski] had no choice,
Because it was a crime,
The strong president is all-knowing and brave.

"The Notorious Ghetto" was composed and sung by Yankele Hershkowitz, and includes a Polish word, *bez-rebotno*. It was written in late 1940 after the ghetto became more organized and new workshops were opened. The first two lines of the song set the scene: At the same time that the inhabitants were laboring and starving, Rumkowski's cronies organized a big party for themselves.

A version of the song is included in *Min Hametsar*, under the title "Der bayrat shpilt in kurtn" (The *Beirat* plays cards) (Blumental 1951 : 139–40), and in Frenkiel's article (1986b : 48). Frenkiel also recalls a slightly different opening of the song:

Di geto du a shteyger
Oyf rumkovski's gasn du.
Zi klapt shoyn vi a zeyger
A sho nokh a sho.
Oy vey, oy vey.

The notorious ghetto
Is here in Rumkowski's streets.
It runs like clockwork
Hour after hour.
Oy vey, oy vey.

The concept which presents the leader Rumkowski and his friends while detailing the suffering of the rest of the ghetto inhabitants is familiar from other songs. The resentment expressed in the lyrics over the ghetto's inequity still reverberates in the singer's mind more than forty years after the fact; this made a powerful impression on me.

The version in song 8 was sung by informants Yaakov Rotenberg and Itka Slodowsky. Yaakov Flam and Yosef Mulaz also contributed fragments of the song, and they remembered a different opening line, one identical to that given in *Min Hametsar* (Blumental 1951 : 139–40). That alternate opening line is:

Czarnieckego *znany,*
Ikh bin zay nisht mekane.

The notorious Czarnieckego,
I do not envy them.

Min Hametsar includes also the following additional verses:

S'iz haynt gite tsaytn,
Me nemt fin ale zaytn.

Czarnieckego *znany,*
Ikh bin zay nisht mekane.

Indzer prezes khayim
Iz a mentsh a khokhem;
Leybn zol froshker,
Er geyt in zayne drokhim.

These are the good times,
One takes as much as he can.
The notorious Czarnieckego,
I do not envy them.

Our president Chaim
Is a clever man;
Long live Froshker,
He follows his ways.

These last two verses shed new light on the meaning of the song overall. Czarnieckego Street was the notorious street where the ghetto prison was located. The singer does not envy the prisoners, who sit while members of the favored authority, the *Beirat,* enjoy the "good life." The *Beirat* would never be punished for its crimes, as long as Chairman Rumkowski is in power; and more than that, even if his power should decline, his successor will probably be worse. Froshker, who is mentioned in the song, was a *Beirat* member in charge of the public kitchens and Rumkowski's most likely successor.

Song 9

Ikh fur kayn palestine (I'm Going to Palestine)

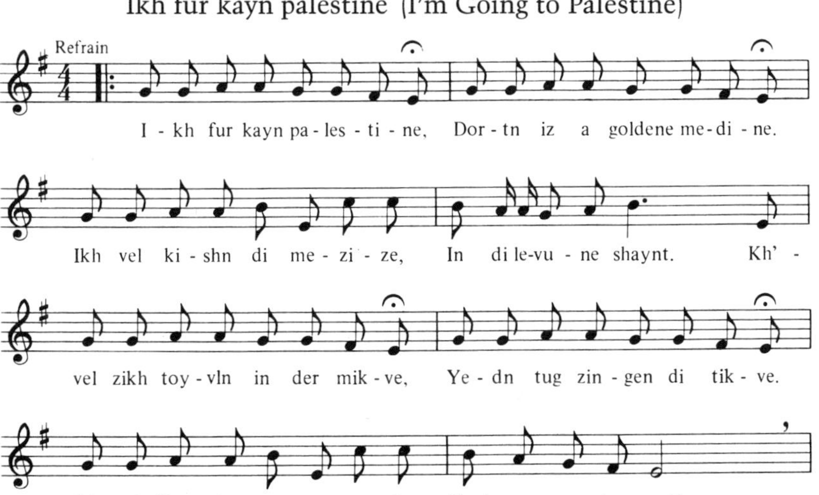

Refren:
Ikh fur kayn palestine,
Dortn iz a goldene medine.
Ikh vel kishn di mezize,
In di levune shaynt.
Kh'vel zikh toyvln in der mikve,
Yedn tug zingen di tikve.
Ikh vel flantsn pomerantsn,

S'vet zayn olerayt!
Ikh vel veyrn dozer in der kehile,
Bentshn esrog in kishn di tfilim,
In reb yoshke kalb
Vet zayn undzer fraynt;
Servus yidn ikh fur ahaym.

Verse:
Di novemyeske gas, oy, oy,
Di sokhrim zenen blat, oy, oy, oy,
Ale zenen haynt shoyn playte;
S'iz dokh nisht kayn shpas.
Rubin mit der zin,
Shmekn dort ahin,
Goldman mit di zibn tekhter,
Moyshe tsiker shmil.
Rumkovski mit zayn armey,
Viln kayn eretz yisruel arayn.
M'vet klapn in polkn,
A gantse tsayt,
A gedile vet zayn, olerayt.

Refren:
Ikh fur kayn palestine . . .

Refrain:
I'm going to Palestine,
That is a golden land.
I will kiss the *mezuzah,*
And the moon will shine.
I'll dip in the *mikveh,*
Every day I'll sing "Hatikvah."
I'll plant oranges,
Everything will be all right!
I'll be active in the community,
I'll bless the *etrog* and kiss the *tfillin,*
And Rabbi Yoshke Kalb
Will be our friend;
Good-bye Jews, I'm going home.

Verse:
The Nowomiejska Street, oy, oy,
The dealers are illegal, oy, oy, oy,
They've all run away by now;
It's not a joke anymore.
Rubin with his son,
Long to go there,
Goldman and his seven daughters,
Moishe Tsiker-Shmil.

Rumkowski and his army,
Want to enter Eretz-Yisrael too.
We'll make noise,
All through that time,
We'll have a celebration, all right!

Refrain:
I'm going to Palestine . . .

This song was composed and performed by Yankele Hershkowitz. It was sung to me by Yaakov Rotenberg, who titled it "A Dream in the Ghetto."[9] The song was sung in the ghetto after a rumor spread that Britain had agreed to let Palestine become the Jewish state. This rumor, as with many others, gave the inhabitants false hope, a feature often transmitted by Yankele Hershkowitz in his topical songs. This song and song 13, "Ikh fur in keltser kant" (I am going to Kielce), share the same melody and poetic form. Interestingly, Yaakov Flam's version mixes the two texts.

"Ikh fur kayn palestine" is laden with Jewish imagery, and includes terms and heroes drawn from tradition and appropriate to the fantasy of the Jewish country described. "I am going to Palestine," says the singer, "that is a golden land." This line possibly alludes to the more stereotypical "land of milk and honey" formulated in Zionist sentiment, wherein Palestine—not America, as described by so many immigrants—is the true golden land. The singer describes his new life: every day he will kiss the *mezuzah* (the inscription on every Jewish doorpost), go to the *mikveh* (ritual bath), and sing "Hatikvah" (Our hope), the national hymn of a free Jewish land. In this "golden land" his life will be dream-bright; he will plant oranges, the moon will shine, he will bathe. The ideas are connected, however, only by the rhyme scheme.

The *esrog* referred to in line ten of the refrain is a special ceremonial fruit from one of four plants blessed during *Sukot* (Feast of Tabernacles), the eight-day holiday commemorating the Israelites' exodus from Egypt. The singer will nevertheless bless the *esrog* every day, or even more often in every prayer (in the second version of the line). And in the free land he will kiss the phylacteries (Heb.: *tfillin*) daily, as a Jew should do.

The last name mentioned in the refrain is not drawn from Jewish custom but from the world of Yiddish literature. Yoshe Kalb is the hero of a novel by I. J. Singer (Isaac Bashevis Singer's older brother), published in 1932 and later adapted into a popular play that was performed throughout America and Europe. Kalb is a Polish Jew who yearns both for women and for God and who finally commits adultery; he disappears, and returns as a different person in the story. The reference to the character in this song is both symbolic and literary; the singer declares, in essence, "Look, once we are free and leave the ghetto we will begin a new life as different, reborn people." In addition, Yoshe Kalb was famous, familiar to all who knew the Yiddish theater. "Look," the singer seems to say, "a famous person will become our friend once we've moved to the golden land, Israel."

The verse describes the passion for Israel felt by everyone; each has a personal reason for wishing to live in Palestine. The black marketeers of Nowomiejska Street, for instance, long to emigrate since everything they do now is illegal and they are not making money anyway. Ordinary people like Rubin and his son want to go, as well as Goldman with his seven daughters, and many others. Even Rumkowski longs to go there with his friends and army of bodyguards. My informant Lucille Eichengreen believes that indeed Rumkowski intended to emigrate to Israel to start a new life once the war had ended.[10]

The last three lines describe the celebration that would take place after the declaration of the independent state of Israel. This prophecy became true only on 29 November 1947, after the inhabitants of the Lodz ghetto had perished.

The melody of "Ikh fur kayn palestine" is in a minor key and common time, while the verse is of a declamatory nature with a great deal of melodic repetition. Intrinsically Jewish is the melodic "filler"—"oy, oy"—of the verse. According to Leo Rosten: "Oy is not a word; it is a vocabulary. It is uttered in as many ways as the utterer's historic ability permits. It is a lament, a protest, a cry of dismay, a reflex of delight. But however sighed, cried, howled, or moaned, oy! is the most expressive and ubiquitous exclamation in Yiddish" (1968 : 277).

According to Beregovski it is common among folksingers to add syllables when there are more pitches than syllables; "usually they add such interjections as *oy* and *oy vey*" (1982 : 40). The ghetto songs continue this Jewish practice.

Song 10

Nor zorgt nisht yidn (Just Don't Worry, Jews)
[Amerike hot erklert] [America Has Declared]

Refren:
Nor zorgt nisht yidn,
In zay tsifridn,
Az indzere tsores vel nemn an ek.
Az got vet geybn,
Mir veln darleybn
Veln mir ale yidn kayn eretz yisruel avek.

Verse 1:
Amerike hot erklert,
Zi makht di velt bakant
Az england miz oyfgeybn
Di yidn dos gantse land.
Men tanst in ale gasn,
In di shtibn iz freylekh,
England shraybt shoyn inter,
Oyf dem nayem yur a meylekh.

Refren:
Nor zorgt nisht yidn . . .

Verse 2:
Mir hobn shoyn eroplanen,
Yidish militer,
Koyln, biksn in harmatn
In mashin gever!

Refren:
Nor zorgt nisht yidn . . .

Refrain:
Just don't worry, Jews,
And be happy,
Our troubles will soon be over.
God willing,
We'll live to see
How we Jews will go to *Eretz-Yisrael.*

Verse 1:
America has declared,
That the world should recognize
That England must let
The Jews have their own country.
In every street there is dancing,
In the houses there is joy,
When England signs the agreement,
For the new year a King.

Refrain:
Just don't worry, Jews . . .

Verse 2:
We will have airplanes,
A Jewish army,
Coal, rifles and artillery
And machine guns!

Refrain:
Just don't worry, Jews . . .

As with the previous song, the topic of this one is the rumored declaration of a Jewish state in British Palestine. *Min Hametsar* gives the phrase "nayem yur a maylekh" at the end of verse 1 as "a nayem Yidishn meylekh," the new Jewish King, which makes more sense in this context (Blumental 1951 : 142). The song was sung in the ghetto by Yankele Hershkowitz, to the same melody as "Kemfn" ("Fight," song 5).

Yaakov Rotenberg calls the song "Amerike hot erklert" (America has declared) "a song of prophecy." The refrain brings comfort and hope and instructs the Jews not to be anxious since, God willing, all Jews will go to *Eretz-Yisrael,* the promised land.

The song introduces the political issue of establishing a Jewish state, as it was stated in the Balfour Declaration of 1917. The song declares that America put pressure on Britain to grant Palestine to the Jews; as a result, the Jews who were already there rejoiced in the streets when the agreement was signed—a fact which historically came about in 1947 with the United Nations' Partition Resolution.

The second verse suggests with some pride the need for a Jewish army in an independent Israel, a pleasant fantasy considering the ghetto audience's total impotence in the face of their current enemies. *Min Hametsar* (in Blumental 1951: 140–42) continues a longer version of this song with an additional issue: Rumkowski's "favoritism," mentioned above in other songs.

The melody of "Nor zorgt nisht yidn" is in a major key and a marching rhythm. My informant performs the refrain-verse of this number in the structural sequence of A B A B′ A. As mentioned before (see discussion of song 5), the original melody comes from David Beyglman's song "Ganovim lid" (Thieves' song), probably a Yiddish theater prewar hit that made its way to the ghetto's street "cabaret."

Song 11

Vayl ikh bin a yidale (Because I Am a Jew)

Refren:
Vayl ikh bin a yidale,
Zing ikh mir dus lidale,
Vayl ikh bin a yid,
Zing ikh mir dos lid.

Verse 1:
Milkhome hot enfangen,
Nisht gehat kayn shtik kolatsie,
Yidelekh hobn ungehoybn
Mit di shpekulatsie.
S'iz bald gevorn a mangel
In zilber drobne gelt,
Gevalt yidn mir hobn milkhome
Oyf der gantse velt.

Refren:
Vayl ikh bin a yidale . . .

Verse 2:
Nishtu a mentsh oyf der velt
Vus vaynt nisht oyf dem khurbn.
Mayn shvester's a froyndine iz oykh gefaln a korbn;
Ikh zey dos bild bay mayne oygn:
Der himl veyet royt,
Sha! a shrapnel iz gefloygn
Trakh dos meydl toyt.

Refren:
Vayl ikh bin a yidale . . .

Verse 3:
Ayner falt fin biksn shos,
Der tsvayter fin shrapneln.
Yetst zeyn di mentshn vi es vert fin a gvir a tel.
Es geyt a yid a fabrikant
Mit a grobn boyekh.
Trakh! a bombe iz gefaln;
Oys fabrikant bloyz royekh.

Refren:
Vayl ikh bin a yidale . . .

Refrain:
Because I am a Jew,
I sing a little song,
Because I am a Jew,
I sing a song.

Verse 1:
When the war started,
We didn't have any dinner,
So Jews started with the speculation.
Immediately there was a shortage
In silver small change,
For heaven's sake: we have a war
Over the entire world.

Refrain:
Because I am a Jew . . .

Verse 2:
There is no one in the world
Who doesn't cry about the destruction.
My sister's friend also became a victim;
I still see the picture before my eyes:
The sky becomes red,
Sha! a shrapnel flew,
Struck the girl dead.

Refrain:
Because I am a Jew . . .

Verse 3:
One is killed by bullets,
The second is killed by shrapnel.
Now people realize how the rich become ruined.
There goes a Jew—a manufacturer
With a great belly.
Crash! A bomb fell;
No more manufacturer, just smoke.

Refrain:
Because I am a Jew . . .

The song was sung to me by Yaakov Rotenberg, and later by Itka Slodowsky, but neither could recall who sang it in the ghetto, nor when they first learned it. Later on, Rotenberg claimed that the song describes the events of the beginning of World War II: "This is what happened on the way to Warsaw. The Germans bombed the roads from the air to clear out the way for the marching German troops approaching Warsaw. Thus, many innocent people were killed on these highways."

Itka Slodowsky attributed the song to Yankele Hershkowitz, but Frenkiel, in his article on Hershkowitz's songs (1986b), makes no mention of this particular composition. This may be because the lyric is from an earlier period, most likely World War I.

The refrain is an ironic commentary on the question "Why do they sing?" The answer follows: "Because I am a Jew." The statement is developed by contrast, each verse reflecting on the innocent refrain, which in turn becomes less innocent and more ironic as the song progresses.

The first verse describes a war which caused all sorts of "speculation" on the part of the Jews. "Gevald" [for heaven's sake], they all cry, "we have a war all over the world."

The second verse stresses the results of the war for the Jews and refers to their common heritage as a source of comfort. Every Jew must mourn and remember the destruction (*khurbn*) of the Temples in Jerusalem. And yet this was not the end of the destruction; more and more victims fell. The verse provides the example of a young girl struck down in the street by flying shrapnel. And yet, although all this is happening, "because I am a Jew I sing a little song." There are no more words to describe catastrophe, no more words to cry out, and therefore I sing! The singer must keep on singing, and the audience must follow his tune.

The third verse concludes with the moral: shrapnel and bombs can hit and kill anyone, rich or poor, fat or thin.

The melody is a "catchy" one (in a minor key) probably of Yiddish folk or theatrical origin. Its short, repetitive motives and the repetition of the symmetrical short refrain make the song easy to remember.

Song 12

Vus zol men tien yidn? (What Shall We Do, Jews?)

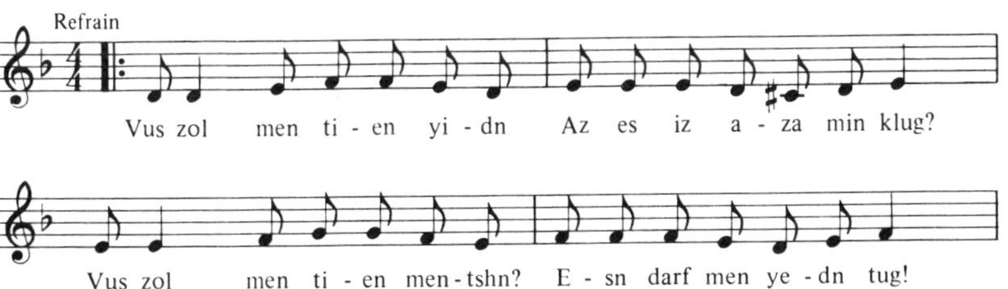

Refren:
Vus zol men tien yidn
Az es iz aza min klug?
Vus zol men tien mentshn?
Esn darf men yedn tug!
Az der mugn vil nisht visn,
Fin kayn geto zakh,
Nor er shrayt in er farlangt
Tsi esn zeyer a sakh.

Verse 1:
S'geyt der libe vinter,
S'falt a shrek a moyre,
M'et nokh pirim zitsn in di sikes,
S'vet zayn simkhes toyre.
Indzer prezes khayim
Iz a mentsh a giter,
M'et nokh in di geto esn
Zemelekh mit piter.

Refren:
Vus zol men tien yidn . . .

Verse 2:
S'geyt der libe vinter
S'falt a shrek a moyre,
Nisht kayn paltn, nisht kayn beged,
S'vet zayn simkhes toyre.
Kh'hob farkoyft di shank shoyn
In di shvigers betn.
S'vet mir starzn broyt in piter
In ferd's flaysh kokletn.

Refren:
Vus zol men tien yidn . . .

Refrain:
What shall we do, Jews
When there is such tragedy?
What shall we do, people?
We have to eat, every day!
Because the stomach doesn't want to know
Anything about our ghetto business,
It only screams and demands
To eat and eat some more.

Verse 1:
Here comes our beloved winter,
Bringing fear and terror,
We'll sit in the *Sukah* for *Purim,*
And celebrate *Simḥat-Torah.*
Our "president" Chaim
Is a good man,
And we'll eat in the ghetto
Rolls with butter.

Refrain:
What shall we do, Jews? . . .

Verse 2:
Here comes our beloved winter
Bringing fear and terror,
No overcoat, no clothes,
Soon it will be *Simḥat-Torah.*
I've already sold the cabinet
And my mother-in-law's bed.
I'll get bread and butter
And horsemeat meatballs.

Refrain:
What shall we do, Jews? . . .

According to Frenkiel (1986b:42–43), this song was composed and sung in the ghetto by Yankele Hershkowitz. I recorded it from Yaakov Rotenberg and Itka Slodowsky separately; however, neither was sure that Hershkowitz was the one to sing it first. A similar version of the song was also published in *Min Hametsar* under the title "Der liber vinter khapt a shrek" (The beloved winter brings fear) (Blumental 1951:140).

The song contains a cynical description of Rumkowski and dates from the early days of the ghetto when people did not have enough work or food. The refrain, which is also included in Frenkiel's article, presents a series of questions with no answers—helpless, hopeless questions: What shall we do when we are hungry and there is no food?

The second part of each verse represents Rumkowski's answer to his hungry masses: One day we shall have bread and butter, meatballs from horsemeat, and also, in Frenkiel's version, eggs and coffee with milk for breakfast.

However, the first part of each verse as recalled by Rotenberg and Slodowsky presents a different idea, one which was perhaps not originally part of this song; it makes use of the same melody and therefore was remembered along with the song. This part mentions some Jewish holidays celebrated topsy-turvy: *Sukot* (the Feast of Tabernacles), *Simḥat-Torah* (the Rejoicing of the Law, following the Feast of Tabernacles), and *Purim* (the carnival festival celebrating the rescue of the Jews in Persia). *Sukot* will last not only eight days but seven months; and in Adar (the sixth month of the Jewish calendar, corresponding to March/April, traditionally the month of multiple rejoicing), instead of celebrating *Purim,* they will celebrate *Simḥat-Torah,* which commemorates the beginning of the Torah cycle reading.

This is the only context in which *Purim* is mentioned. *Purim* itself, with its carnival, costumes, and plays, was never celebrated in the ghetto. It is a tradition in *Purim* to represent opposites dramatically: a man will play a woman, a youth an old man. But in the ghetto, where normal life was reversed to begin with, would a *Purimshpiel* (a *Purim* play, the "father" of the Yiddish theater) signify a return to normalcy? The ghetto was clearly not the place for games and plays presenting absurdity, since life itself was absurd.

In general "Vus zol men tien yidn" describes the poverty of the inhabitants, who end up selling all their belongings in order to get food, and yet they remained hungry.

Min Hametsar's version (Blumental 1951:46) adds three lines which include a complaint about the nine Marks the unemployed inhabitants received in order to buy food rations, an amount that was, of course, insufficient for survival.

The melody of the verse resembles the melody of the refrain of a well-known folksong titled "Tsen brider" (Yidd.: Ten brothers). The original song describes the fate of nine brothers who died leaving the last one to sing before he starves (see Mlotek and Mlotek 1988: 121–22). This song inspired another poet during the Holocaust to set new lyrics to that melody (see Kalisch 1985:48–57); however, there is no reference to the original context in this song.

Song 13

Ikh fur in keltser kant (I'm Going to Kielce)

Refren:
Ikh fur in keltser kant,
Dort est men retekhlekh mit shmant,
Mayrn, burkes far a drayer,
Khutsi khinem krigt men ayer.
Dort iz s'leybn iz nisht tayer,
Fur avek zay nisht kayn frayer.
Ikh fur in keltser kant,
Dort est men retekhlekh mit shmant.

Verse:
Dort boyet zekh a naye medine,
Mit in ven zayen mer kayn grine.
Rumkovski khayim vet zayn indzer fraynt.
Servus yidn servus,
Ikh fur nokh haynt!

Refren:
Ikh fur in keltser kant . . .

Refrain:
I'm going to Kielce,
Where they eat radishes with sweet cream,
Carrots, beets as much as you want,
And eggs for half the price.
Life there is not expensive,
Go there, do not be a fool.
I'm going to Kielce,
Where radishes and sweet cream they eat.

Verse:
There, they are building a new nation,
And nobody there will be "green."
Rumkowski Chaim will be our friend.
Bye-Bye Jews,
I'm going right now!

Refrain:
I'm going to Kielce . . .

According to Frenkiel (1986b:44), this song was also composed and sung by Yankele Hershkowitz in the ghetto, although the version he includes in his article is slightly different from the present one. The melody and the structure of the song are similar to those of "Ikh fur kayn palestine" (I'm going to Palestine) (song 9). Some lines of this song are also included in *Min Hametsar*'s version of "Klert nisht yidn" (Don't worry, Jews) (Blumental 1951:141).

This is yet another commentary on a rumor that spread throughout the ghetto, namely that in the region of Kielce, Jews lived free and had plenty to eat, just as before the war.

The song mentions food, the most desirable commodity in the ghetto where there never was enough to eat. Its description of food is realistic but its imaginings border on raw cynicism when it describes the new nation led by a "friendly" Rumkowski.

Yaakov Flam sings a combination of Rotenberg's and Frenkiel's version and the refrain of "Ikh fur kayn palestine":

S'iz a moda aroys
Az fin klayn biz groys,
Mir hobn du a yetser hore,
In mir viln aroys.
Mir hobn a yidish land,
Mir veln du tapn a vant,
Yedn tug meltn kozes
Un me't tsipn shmant.
Yedn tug zugn a bisl thilim . . .

Ikh fur nokh keltser kant
Dort est men retekhlekh mit shmant,
Tsibl mayrn far a tsvayer,
B'khatsi khinem krigt men ayer.
Dortn s'lebn iz a mekhaye,
Dortn iz du vus tsi kayen,
Dortn nishtu kayn geyler band,
Rumkovski's geto land.

It is a new style
That everyone, small and big,
Has the evil passion,
And we want out.
We have a Jewish land,
We will have a feast,
Every day we will milk goats
And will drink sweet cream.
Every day you recite some psalms.
[Variant continues as in song 9, line 10,
to end of refrain.]

I'm going to Kielce
Where radish and sweet cream they eat,
Onions, carrots as much as you want,
And eggs for half the price.
Life there is heaven,
There is something to chew there,
There is not a yellow band,
And not Rumkowski's ghetto-land.

This song makes it clear that the people are desperate to leave the ghetto; they have "the evil passion," just as if the devil had got into them. They want to live in a free Jewish land where they would not have to wear the hated yellow star.

The melody is of Jewish origin; its minor modality and melodic repetitions are, according to Idelsohn (1967:398–400), characteristic of Yiddish folksong. Minor modality was less pointedly "ethnic" in Eastern Europe than it was later in the "new country"—America—where it became one of the major symbols for Jewish popular music (Slobin 1980 and 1982). As Beregovski observed (1982:294), the Ashkenazic Jews shared minor-mode predilections with their medieval Rhineland neighbors and, later and eastward, with the various Slavic peoples among whom they settled. However, since ethnic identity was not an issue in the ghetto, relying on traditional familiar trends provided comfort to the singer and his audience.

Song 14

Es geyt a yeke (It's a Yeke Walks Around)

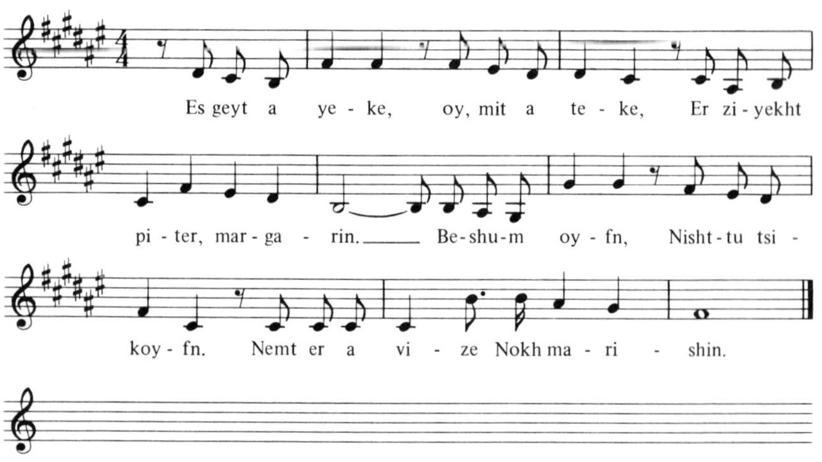

Es geyt a yeke, oy,
Mit a teke.
Er ziyekht piter, margarin.
Beshum oyfn,
Nishtu tsi koyfn.
Nemt er a vize
Nokh marishin.

It's a *yeke* walks around, oy,
With his briefcase.
Looks for butter, margarine.
No way, nowhere,
Can he buy it.
So he takes a 'visa'
To Marysin.

Yeke, as observed above, was a nickname given to the German Jews. Leo Rosten characterizes the term in his book *The Joys of Yiddish* as "Origin unknown, A German [Jew]" (1968:468). Philip Bohlman treats the name and its meaning at length in his book *"The Land Where Two Streams Flow"*: "The exact meaning of *Yeke* may vary according to social and linguistic background. . . . Eastern European Jews were probably the first to apply the term to German Jews. . . . Another possible source stems from the era of emancipation, when German Jews abandoned the traditional long frock of orthodoxy for the shorter jacket, or *Jacke,* worn by non-Jews . . ." (1989:19–21). Like the *Yeke* in Israel, the subject of Bohlman's investigation, the *Yeke* in the ghetto had problems of adjustment.

At the close of the summer of 1941, Jews from Germany, Austria, Czechoslovakia, and Luxembourg were brought to the ghetto. The *Chronicle* describes in numerous entries the tragedy of these Western European Jews. The chronicler also makes the following comment on the song in his entry of 5 December 1941:

> *Es Geyt a Yeke Mit A Teke,* so runs the refrain of the ghetto's latest hit song, which is sung to the tune of the popular army song "The Machine Gun." It makes fun of the adventures of the newly arrived "Germans" (that is, German Jews), popularly known in Yiddish slang here as *yekes.* The song treats their ups and downs with good humor and tells of the *yekes,* forever hungry and searching for food, and the "locals" who make fun of them and quite often take advantage of their naivete and unfamiliarity with local customs. The song is about women in pants parading through the streets of Bałut. The author and performer of this song is the popular ghetto street "troubadour" Hershkowitz. (Dobroszycki 1984:92)

From this description it appears that a further verse concerning "women parading" was lost. I was able, however, to recover the refrain, and this part of the song was remembered by quite a few of my informants.

The chronicler points out the tragedy within a tragedy, that of the German Jews in the ghetto who were culturally apart and unable to adjust to a new set of conditions. In the ghetto it was noticeable that the *yekes* had different manners, clothes, and education; they therefore had a very difficult time adjusting and integrating with the Jews native to Lodz. Unlike their Eastern European brethren, who were used to shortages and poor hygienic conditions even before the war, these Western Jews came from a comfortable, bourgeois environment. Most of them perished shortly after arriving in the ghetto.

Yaakov Flam describes the tragedy of the German Jews: "They ate what they had the moment they got it; they could not make a loaf of bread last seven days, as all the others knew how, so they ate it all on the first day, and then stayed hungry. After a short time they all died."

All my informants remember the German Jews and cannot forget their tragedy. Most of them recall this song, or at least that there was such a song. I have noted as many renditions of this song as of the popular "Rumkowski Chaim" song, namely, fifteen versions.

Yankele Hershkowitz, too, was sympathetic to the plight of the German Jews, yet treats their destiny as a source of humor. When the *yeke* cannot obtain decent food, for example, he "takes a visa to Marysin." Marysin was the forest area in Lodz where the graveyard was located, and this was the final resting place of the German Jews.

Khane Mlotek suggests that the melody stems from a Yiddish folksong and not from the popular marching tune (mentioned in the *Chronicle* without further details).[11] Khane finds similarities between "Es geyt a yeke" and "Fort a kholutsl" (A pioneer goes away).

Song 15

Nishtu kayn przydziel (There Are No Coupons)

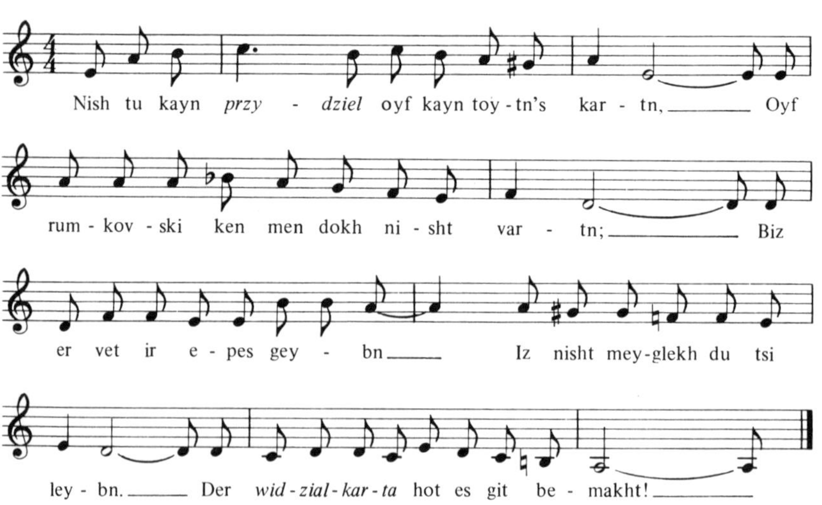

Refren:
Nishtu kayn *przydziel* oyf kayn toytn's kartn,
Oyf rumkovski ken men dokh nisht vartn;
Biz er vet ir epes geybn
Iz nisht meyglekh du tsi leybn.
Der *widzial-karta* hot es git gemakht!

Verse:
Di shaynuvna iz geveysn shvarts a sekretarn,
A dike dame und a fete, haynt vet zi shoyn darn.
Gehat hot zi nor kartn fir
Gegesn hot zi on a shie.
Haynt hot zi kayn kartn shoyn mer nisht.

Refrain:
There are no food coupons for a dead person's cards,
For Rumkowski one cannot wait;
By the time he gives us anything
We won't be alive any more.
The Main Office is doing very well!

Verse:
The Shaynuvna was Schwartz's secretary,
A fat and heavy lady, only now she's quite skinny.
She accumulated four cards
And ate without limit.
Now she has cards no more.

This song is a contrafact on "Papirosn" (Cigarettes) (Mlotek and Mlotek 1988:267–69), one of the most popular songs of the Yiddish theater. Its lyrics tell of an orphan forced to earn his sustenance by selling cigarettes in the streets of a nameless Eastern European city. At the end of the song, the young hero bewails the fate that awaits him: "Nobody wants to buy from me! I will waste to nothing and die like a dog." The scenario was familiar to Herman Yablokoff, who wrote both the lyrics and the music to the song, as it certainly must have been to the ghetto audience, most of whom had suffered enormous deprivation during World War I. Yablokoff (1968/69, 2:202ff.) writes that he composed the song in Europe in the mid-1920s; however, it gained popularity only upon its American publication in 1932.

One can only speculate as to whether the Lodz ghetto version of "Papirosn" was inspired primarily by the catchy tune or the lugubrious lyric content. However, the song was popular throughout the system of ghettos and camps, where other parodies were written. In the Vilna ghetto, Rikle Glezer wrote new lyrics on the fate of the inhabitants being sealed in the ghetto and then killed in Ponar, under the title "Es iz geven a zumertog" (It was a summer day) (see Kaczerginsky 1948:7–8 and 364). In the Warsaw ghetto the melody used was from a song titled "Di broyt farkoyferin" (The breadseller), describing the fate of a starving orphan (Kaczerginsky 1948:110–11 and 364). On the recording made by the Historical Committee of

Munich, 1946, the song describes the fate of the Jews of Sosnowiec under the title "Amol a heym" (Once upon a time a home).[12]

The Lodz version was composed by Yankele Hershkowitz. It does not refer to a specific tragedy, but rather treats the ongoing lack of food in the ghetto with grim humor. The situation depicted concerned the issuance of food ration coupons (the Polish slang *przydziel*) to certified workers by the ghetto's Office of Food Distribution (the Polish *widzial-karta*). These certificates were naturally in great demand, so much so that when a worker died, his surviving colleagues vied for them. (The *Chronicle* for 11 June 1943 reports that "a group of Jews obtained food illegally by using ration cards of people who had been resettled" [i.e., died] (Dobroszycki 1984:345). Many other stories have come down to us about families concealing the bodies of their loved ones in order to ensure a continuing supply of the deceased's food coupons.

Yaakov Flam recalled that the incident described in the song took place, in all probability, in 1942. According to Flam, the heroine, Shaynuvna, worked in the Food Distribution Office, where she devised a self-serving method of staying well-fed. Rather than hand over workers' death certificates to the proper authorities, she kept them for herself, accumulating the rights to four persons' rations (in one version of the song) before being caught. The punishment for her "white-collar" crime was assignment to the despised occupation of *fecalist* (gutter sweeper).

My primary source for "Nishtu kayn przydziel" was Yehiel Frenkiel, who rejoiced at Shaynuvna's punishment. Interestingly, Flam perceived Shaynuvna more as a heroic outlaw who managed to outwit the authorities—at least for a time. This is clear in an alternate version of the refrain which I received from him:

Refren:
Men nemt a *przydziel* oyf tsvay toytn's kartn.
Vus toyg mir oyf rumkovski's ratsye vartn?
Men nemt a *przydziel* oyf tsvay toytn's
In di zonder blaybt a shoyte,
Az *widzial-karta* iz oykh narish geven.

Refrain:
One takes a food coupon good for two cards of death.
What good is it to wait for Rumkowski's cards?
One takes the food coupon for two cards of death
And fools the Jewish Police,
And the main distribution office also looks foolish.

Song 16
A pensjonat (The Boardinghouse)

Verse 1:
A *pensjonat* gevolt oy makhn,
Oy vey,
A *pensjonat* gevolt oy makhn,
Fresn, zoyfn, in oplakhn,
Oy vey, oy vey,
Fresn, zoyfn, in oplakhn,
Oy vey, oy vey, oy vey.

Verse 2:
A *pensjonat* an idilye,
Oy vey,
A *pensionat* an idilye,
Mit muzik un mit a vilye,
Oy vey, oy vey,
Mit muzik un mit a vilye,
Oy vey, oy vey, oy vey.

Verse 1:
A boardinghouse they decided to build,
Oy vey,
A boardinghouse they decided to build,
Eat, swill, and laugh,
Oy vey, oy vey,
Eat, swill, and laugh,
Oy vey, oy vey, oy vey.

Verse 2:
A boardinghouse, exclusive,
Oy vey,
A boardinghouse, exclusive,
With music and villa,
Oy vey, oy vey,
With music and villa,
Oy vey, oy vey, oy vey.

The English word "boardinghouse" is not exactly equivalent to the Polish-German-Yiddish word *pensjonat* in this context. Therefore, I have left the Polish word in the Yiddish version to stand for its original meaning as a recreation center or a rest home.

This song, which also was composed and sung by Yankele Hershkowitz, was recorded from Yosef Mulaz[13] and Yeḥiel Frenkiel (1986b: 51). It is a parody on a Yiddish folksong, "Af di felder, grine felder" (Over the greenfields, on the plain) (Rubin 1965: 8), and it uses the inner refrain of that song, "oy vey." It is the only song composed by Yankele that paraphrases an original song. The original ballad, written by the well-known Yiddish poet Zalman Shneor, tells about a soldier dying somewhere in the green fields during World War I, and asking a bird not to tell his mother of his death.

This song is a critique of the *Beirat,* which in 1941 built a *pensjonat,* a recreation center of a sort, in the green fields of Marysin. Marysin also contained the orphanages and youth organization centers as well as the cemetery. The *Beirat* members did not know shortages, while in contrast the ghetto dwellers went hungry. They did not feel guilty or ashamed, however, tasting the "good life" within the ghetto. As stated in the *Chronicle* of 15 July 1941: "Ghetto high life spends weekends in Marysin . . . or otherwise, God forbid, they might not be considered part of the elite" (Dobroszycki 1984: 67).

Yosef Mulaz described this as a "tragic song." He remarked: "When I recalled it before the interview, I cried and cried and was not sure even I would be able to sing it to you."

In the boardinghouse, as described in the first recorded verse, the *Beirat* members eat and laugh. The second verse informs us of the high standards of living they enjoyed. All the lines rhyme, except for the "oy vey, oy vey," which was the experience of the dwellers: pain. The theme underlying the ballad is that of death.

Frenkiel adds three more verses to the song (1986b: 51). In his final verse the singer presents himself: he too was invited to live in Marysin, "in a hole dug in the ground."

Song 17

Street Cry for Saccharine

Sakharin finf a marek,
Sakharin originele,
Orginele, orginele,
Sakharin orginele,
Sakharin orginele,
Sakharin finf a marek.

Saccharine, five for one Mark,
Saccharine, like new,
Like new, like new,
Saccharine, like new,
Saccharine, like new,
Saccharine, five for one Mark.

Variant A

Street Cry for Saccharine and Taffy

Sakharinke, tofi,
Orginele, tofi,

Seks a tseyne, sakharin,
Seks a tseyne, sakharin,
Kletser zoylen,
Gantse baylen,
Orginele, tofi,
Sakharinkes, tofi.

Saccharine, taffy,
Like new, taffy,
Six for ten—saccharine,
Six for ten—saccharine,
By the fistful,
A whole clench,
Like new, taffy,
Saccharine, taffy.

Variant B

Street Cry for Saccharine and Taffy

Sakharin, sakharin,
Orginele sakharin,
Seks a tseyne,
Di gite kilove,
Di vibrove,
Di vibrove,
Di gantse broytn,
Di gantse kletser,
Tsikerlekh, tofis, tofis.

Saccharine, saccharine,
Like new saccharine,
Six for ten,
A good kilo,
The best,
The best,
Like a loaf of bread,
Like a nice long log,
Candies, taffy, taffy.

Most of my informants remembered several versions of this cry, the call of children standing on street corners advertising their meager products.

The first version was recorded from Yaakov Bressler, who came to the Lodz ghetto in August 1942. As he was still quite young (about thirteen years old) he sought to support himself by selling saccharine on the streets, a common means of earning a living for poor and orphaned youth. He remembered the words and the tune of this song very clearly.

The second version was recorded from Yosef Mulaz, who also recalled the going price of saccharine. The price of commodities such as saccharine varied in accordance with the inevitable laws of supply and demand (even in the ghetto); this accounts for the disparity in price in his rendition. The third version, which is similar to the second one, was recorded from Yeḥiel Frenkiel. (Chava Rosenfarb includes in her trilogy the same version that Frenkiel recalls [1972, 2:183].) Particularly in the second version, the street peddler sings his product's praises with hyperbolic license: he boasts that the taffy feels as good in the customer's mouth as newly soled shoes would feel on his feet.

Numerous other informants remembered this street cry as well as the poor, ragged peddlers standing in the streets with their saccharine or candies wrapped in small conical bits of paper. Because the peddlers feared both the police and the legitimate Jewish businessmen, their lives and livelihood were constantly in danger. However, they continued to sing out of an inner artistic impulse or simply until their merchandise had all been sold.

Street cries have been known worldwide and through recorded history, but in the ghetto the commercial call was laden with emotional overtones generated by the unique context. Saccharine—the sugar substitute—is not an especially inspiring commodity in ordinary times. In the ghetto, however, a song advertising its virtues was a symbol of what life had become: no family, no food, no choice.

The chronicler Oskar Rosenfeld recorded in his entry of 7 August 1943: "The sun is white-hot. The gutters are dry. There is not even a tuft of cloud in the sky. In the streets, the boys cry 'Saccharine here!' and 'Toffee here!' . . . Onions are a rarity in the ghetto like so much else" (Dobroszycki 1984:366).

The version transcribed was the one sung by Yaakov Bressler; other versions contained only fragments of the musical motive.

Song 18

Az men geyt oyf dem brik
(When One Goes on the Bridge)

Az men geyt oyf dem brik
Meg men goymel bentshn
Az der brik zol nisht aynfaln
Mit di mentshn.

When one goes on the bridge
He should pray *hagomel*

That the bridge won't break
With all the people.

These four lines were recited to me by Yaakov Flam, who could not recall the melody. The three bridges in Lodz were quite significant since they linked the two segments of the ghetto which were located in different parts of the city. Most of the people had to cross a bridge twice a day, to and from work. The bridges were crowded and the Germans carefully supervised the traffic. Thus, crossing a bridge successfully symbolized having made it through another hard day. The song says that because of the crowds and the hazards encountered, the traveler, once safely across, should recite the *ha'gomel,* the prayer offered in thanks for surviving a life-threatening crisis.

Bridges again figure in a song by the poet Miriam Harel, whose emotional turning point in the ghetto occurred while she observed German soldiers from one of the bridges in Lodz (see song 23).

Summary

In the eighteen street songs, I discerned four dominant themes, which I will summarize in descending order of frequency of appearance: hunger or food; corrupt administration and abuse of power, hope for freedom, and a call for revolt.

The theme of hunger dominates all the street songs. This theme is paramount in other genres of ghetto songs as well, as I will show later in this work. Four songs out of the eighteen speak directly about hunger, and five others describe food. Two refer to the subject of hunger by talking about the theft of food, or food coupons (something relatively rare in normal times).

A second prominent theme in the songs is the criticism of the Jewish authorities and their abuse of power. These authorities were the cause of suffering, in the eyes of the inhabitants. Their grief and anger had no avenue for expression except through these songs. Five songs speak mainly of the abuse of power, while others mention it indirectly.

The third dominant theme in the songs is hope. The inhabitants expressed their hope for a better future, which gave them the will to continue living in the ghetto. The fourth theme, a call for revolt which expresses both anger and hope, also appears in two songs. When no outside support for an armed revolt—or ammunition for such a revolt—was feasible, the song became the only weapon.

The writers expressed their grief and anger using sarcasm, cynicism, and humor. Yet, although obsessed with their suffering and hunger, cut off from any sources of information, they still had hope.

On the other hand, the street cries—functional calls for commerce—speak in that context of hunger and fear (as in the last song).

The street songs serve as a mirror of life in the ghetto, expressing the survivors' experiences. These songs also act as a movable cabaret to relate the story of the ghetto with scenes that are both humanistic and sensitive.

As noted by the survivors and in written sources, the majority of the ghetto street songs were sung to preexisting melodies. The contrafact technique can be recognized in most of the songs in which the musical phrases were stretched to accommodate the new text. Yet only two songs (nos. 15 and 16) are parodies in which the original tunes can be recognized; these form a subtext to the new lyrics and speak of a new reality.

Contrafact seems to have been used because the supply of melodies could not meet the demand of new lyrics, and thus old melodies were harnessed for this purpose. It also means that, in this genre, the main innovations lie in the texts and not in the music.

Most of the songs are contrafact on earlier Yiddish songs. Two songs are probably derived from popular march tunes. In their new use, the marching rhythms symbolize the Jewish resistance, protest, and existence. One Polish popular tune—a tango—was also used to recall memories of normal times when the Jews were part of Polish society and shared their popular culture. The tango perhaps evoked nostalgic memories, apart from its topical lyrics.

From a musicological point of view, there is a correlation between the mode used and the source. Thus, of the eighteen songs from the repertoire I analyzed, ten are in a minor mode and mainly of Jewish origin, five are in a major mode, and two are in the augmented minor second scale. Since the predilection for the minor key is a well-known trait in Yiddish music, this aspect of the ghetto repertoire falls within the framework of an overall "national" song style. However it should be remembered that within the ghetto, the important elements of this genre were the sung poetry, the text and its performance.

NOTES

1. The interview was conducted in Hebrew, in Yaakov Rotenberg's home at Givatagim, 28 August 1985.

2. David Beyglman (referred to elsewhere in this work) composed a song

on the fate of the Gypsies. The song coincides with Yaakov's moving account. See song 33.

3. The Yiddish dialect of Lodz is different from the Lithuanian dialect which had become the standard orthography for new literary writings and professional performance, as dictated by the YIVO institute in 1936.

4. In the refrain, *getunya* is a Slavic diminutive for "ghetto," ironic in this context. The song includes many other Polish slang words.

5. Interview with Itka Slodowsky, Bat-Yam, 10 September 1985.

6. Letter from Khane Mlotek to author, September 1989.

7. Beregovski devoted several essays to the question of the *frigish* and augmented second and their meanings. For a detailed discussion see Beregovski 1982: 294–302. Slobin (1980, 1982) also has documented the symbolic meaning of the *frigish* and augmented second scale for the Jews.

8. Interview with Freda Burns, Los Angeles, 24 March 1986.

9. Another time Rotenberg sang "by yeder *tfilah*" (in every prayer) in line 10 of the refrain, instead of "kishn di tfilim" (kiss the *tfillim*); the same version appears in Frenkiel's article (1986b: 44–45).

10. Interview with Lucille Eichengreen, Berkeley, California, 17 April 1986.

11. Letter from Khane Mlotek to author, September 1989.

12. The earliest recordings known to me were done by the Historical Committee for War Crimes in Munich in 1946. These recordings are poorly documented, though they serve as a source for Kaczerginsky's anthology (1948) and Gelman's article (1985). The recordings are at the National Sound Archives in Jerusalem, and I refer to them when relevant. For a further discussion of ghetto versions of "Papirosn," see Gila Flam and Bret Werb, "Old Schmaltz in New Bottles" (forthcoming).

13. Interview with Yosef Mulaz, Kiryat Bialik, 28 March 1985.

4

Domestic Songs

I have known Miriam Harel since my childhood. She was one of my father's friends from the Gordonya Youth Organization in Lodz. When I was seeking Yiddish singers for the purposes of my research, my father recommended Miriam. He remembered her beautiful voice and her singing for the young people in Lodz. Thus a meeting was arranged.

Miriam's ghetto songs, interwoven with her life story, strongly impressed me as examples of personal expression as well as means for survival during times of great psychological stress. These experiences of a woman who endured despair and yet retained hope deserve to be remembered.

In this chapter I will introduce the ghetto songs Miriam composed, mainly in Polish, between 1941 and 1945. In order to preserve these songs she reconstructed them in Italy after her liberation in 1945, while awaiting permission to immigrate to Israel.[1]

Miriam's Story

Miriam Harel, née Mary Goldberg, was born in Lodz in November 1924. She lived in the ghetto from March 1940 to August 1944, and on leaving it she was sent to Auschwitz. She cannot recall exactly how long she was in Auschwitz, only that she was there. Later, she was sent to work in a factory in France but soon was shipped east to the camp at Bergen-Belsen. From Bergen-Belsen, finally, she was sent to the labor camp in Muhltuer. Then, in April 1945, she was liberated by the American army. After liberation she returned to Lodz to look for her family. Of her immediate family, including her parents, six brothers and sisters, uncles, aunts, and cousins, only two of her older sisters survived. Miriam, who has been living in Israel since 1948, is married and has three children.

Miriam remembers the happy days of her childhood. Her father was a rabbinical judge and her mother ran a women's clothing store. She attended elementary school and had completed the first year of high school before the war. She recalls vividly the events and sounds of the ghetto: the shouting of mothers when their babies were taken away, the crying of children begging for a piece of bread, and the sounds of nature—the cold winds blowing and the hushed falling of snow.

In the ghetto, Miriam felt the need to express herself in words. She had to record what she had seen, felt, and thought. As she says, "I had to release the anger." She wrote for herself but also for posterity, since she was not sure that she was going to survive. By 1941, when one of her cousins escaped from a transport, she knew that the people being removed from the ghetto were going to their deaths.

Her first ghetto audience consisted of her sisters, who encouraged her to read her writings for the rest of the family. She adapted familiar melodies to some of her poems in order to entertain her family during the cold, dark ghetto evenings.

In addition she showed some of her writings to her friend Pnina (who did not survive) in order to receive some feedback and critical comments. Miriam does not consider her poetry to be "high literature"; she offers apologies every time she shows someone her writings. She does, however, acknowledge poetry's significance in her life, the role it serves for her listeners, as well as its historical importance. "People should know what we went through, otherwise they will not believe us. They will think that we are mad." And indeed, at least until the trial of Adolf Eichmann (1962), many people even in Israel chose not to believe in the stories of the Holocaust survivors, an attitude that led to silence on the part of many concerning past events.

Miriam studied Polish and knows the language very well, but she also studied Hebrew and continued Hebrew studies both at home and in the youth organization to which she belonged (Gordonya). However, she did not express herself in Hebrew until she settled in Israel. She understood a little Yiddish, but because of her Polish education she chose not to write in that language. After liberation, while waiting in Italy for permission to immigrate to Israel, she met survivors from various ghettos and camps who chided her for not knowing how to speak or write Yiddish. She then took up the study of that language, composed a poem in it, and even translated some poetry from Polish into Yiddish. All her other poems, written in the ghetto in Polish, were reconstructed from memory during her stay in Italy after the liberation.

Miriam also kept a diary for three years, but she burned it when her family learned that the *Gestapo* had deported a family upon discovering a diary kept by one of the girls.

In 1940 she was a member of the Gordonya *Hakhsharah* and lived in Marysin in its camp. This was her happiest time in the ghetto, and she remembers the songs and dances of the Gordonya youth. Beginning in 1941 she worked in a factory, stitching buttons on German army coats.

Miriam has written prose and poetry ever since she learned the alphabet. She comes from a musical family, loves to sing, and has a pleasant voice. She sang in choirs and later was a soloist for her youth organization's activities. She explained her reason for setting her poems to known melodies: "I needed a rhythmical framework. Maybe I did not know how to write a rhythmical poem by myself, so I used a known one as a defense."

Miriam describes her compositions: "The words were lying in the streets, you just had to pick them up. It was not my imagination, the words were there; I just had to put them on paper. I knew the melodies from before the war. All the melodies were happy melodies, I did not know any sad melodies. So I wrote, and I felt very free after I let it out. My family read it, then sang it according to the melodies again and again. These were long, dark nights and we were all hungry and could not fall asleep."

Miriam explains the role of singing in this way: "Singing had an important role in Jewish life. The Jewish people came to such a deep state of despair that only singing could help. When one sings, even when he sings a sad song, his loneliness disappears, he listens to his own voice. He and his voice become two people. Singing is a manifestation of hope. People before their deaths do not mourn, they sing. The song is a cry, and afterwards you feel free."

The following seven poems composed by Miriam Goldberg Harel during her ghetto confinement describe the period 1941–45. The first poem was written in Polish, translated into Hebrew by Miriam for the purpose of this book, and later incorporated into her own published memoir; I have now translated it into English.[2]

Song 19

Jeden dzień w getcie

Ojciec się kiwa nad gemarą,
Ciągle zaczyna na nowo.
Wielką ma pewność, silną ma wiarę
Że cud jakiś zrobi Jehowa.

Matka się krząta koło jedzenia:
To tylko zupa jest wodna.
Nikt nie zrozumie głębi cierpienia
Matki, co dzieci jej głodne.

Siostra ceruje pończochę starą,
Braciszek spogląda w rycine,
Wszyscy wdychamy zupy parę
I połykany slinę.

Wysoko, na szafie schowany, kusi
Mały bochenek chleba
Dla całej rodziny starczyć musi:
Dla wygłodzonych ust siedem.

Dwa lichtarze i modlitewnik
I święte biblie, tak drogie
Stoją na półce sciennej, drzewnej,
Każą się modlić do Boga.

Siedzę przy oknie z szybą złamaną
I patrzę nav błotną ulicę.
Marzę o kraju słońcem skąpanym,
O złotym polu pszenicy.

Wiem, że gdzieś, daleko za morzem
Jest kraj, gdzie Żydem być wolno.
Gdzie chłop żydowski ziemię orze,
Orkę, drogą, gna, polną.

Dzieci żydowskie zdrowe, wesołe,
Na obiad wołają matki.
Palmy słaniają cień dookoła,
W ogrodach pachną kwiatki.

Fale Jordanu rytmem płyną
Tam, w dalekiej krainie.
A tutaj naród cały ginie
Marząc o Palestynie.

Tu, w getcie, giną ostatnie już
Potomki Jehudy Makabi.
Za drutem stoi niemiecki stróż
Gotowy strzelać i zabić.

Śnieg pada z deszczem zmieszany,
Niebo ołowiem grozi.
Wiatr miota oknem złamanym
Oddech i koście mrozi.

Tato wciąż jeszcze siedzi nad gemarą,
Mama przytula swe dzieci.

Siostra ceruje pończochę starą,
Znów minął dzień jeden w getcie.

A Day in the Ghetto (a poem)—1941

Father sways over his *gemara,*
Starts and stops again and again.
He believes in God,
God will make a miracle.

Mother walks circles around the food:
Only a pot of watery soup.
No one can believe the powerful suffering
Of a mother whose children are starving.

A sister is sewing an old sock,
A brother is staring at a picture,
We all breathe soap steam
And swallow spit.

Up there, in the closet, is hidden
A small loaf of bread
Which has to feed the whole family:
Seven hungry mouths.

A couple of candlesticks and a prayer book
And the dearest Torah books
Stand on a dark wood shelf,
Asking us to pray to God.

I sit next to a table with a broken glass
And look at the street, full of mud.
I dream that somewhere is a land full of sun,
Somewhere, a field of golden wheat.

I know that far away beyond the sea
There is a country where a Jew can live.
And a farmer can farm his land
And push the plow.

Jewish children, healthy and happy,
Are called to lunch by their mother.
Palms spread their cooling shade around,
And in the gardens, perfumed flowers.

The Jordan's waves flow in rhythm
There in that faraway land.
But here, all our people have been destroyed
While dreaming of the land of Israel.

Here in the ghetto the last are disappearing,
Offspring of Judas Maccabaeus.

Behind a barbed-wire fence, a German guard is standing
Ready to shoot and kill.

Snow is falling mixed with rain,
The gray skies are threatening.
The wind shakes a broken window
And freezes the bones and the soul.

Father is still bowed over his *gemara,*
Mother hugs her children.
A sister is sewing an old sock,
Another day passed in the ghetto.

In the poem Miriam describes the beginning of her personal tragedy in the ghetto. When she reads it today, the poem sounds naive and simplistic to her, but at the time she wrote it she was trying to capture some complex feelings. This poem was her response to the arrival of autumn, with its promise of a difficult winter to follow, no food, and a living situation growing worse every day.

The poem describes the suffering of her family from a child's perspective, but a child who can see the weakness of her parents and wants to protect them. According to Miriam's interpretation of her poem:

> I, the child, could not help, but could provide comfort by singing that this was not the end, and the future had to be better. Children are more optimistic, they are more naive, they do not understand what death is, therefore they believe that bad times will go away. We children observed and remember and recall, but at that time we did not exactly understand what it meant. When I saw announcements in the ghetto for people to register for work, and I knew that it meant that they will never come back, I came home and told my parents: "I saw an announcement that tomorrow they will give away potatoes." I knew in a sense that I had to encourage them. My parents were so weak they could not even move out of their beds, and we the children were stronger and felt we had to encourage them; we had to believe and hope for better times.

In this poem she describes her father and mother and the conflict of beliefs between them and herself. Miriam remembers her father, a pious Jew who believed in God and the Torah and obeyed all the *taryag mitzvot,* the 613 precepts of the Torah, until his dying moment. Miriam, on the other hand, respected her father's ways, but chose her own path very early in her life, becoming a member of a Zionist organization. She talks about this conflict of beliefs: "Father was against any Zionist movement as he believed that only the Messiah should bring us back to Israel. And about Herzl [the founder of the political form of Zionism] he did not talk nicely. But I went to Gordonya and learned an opposite view, so I got a twisted picture of the world."

For Miriam the symbol of her father is the *gemara,* the commentaries on the *mishnah,* the code of the Jewish law dating from the third century A.D. Her father held to his familiar world of books, and by so doing escaped from the horrors of reality. He believed, and died with his beliefs intact.

Miriam vividly described the hunger in the ghetto: "The greatest enemy of every creature was hunger. Hunger was the greatest killer, very efficient and quick. After a short time people lost weight, lost their health, and gave up hope."

When she recalls her father and the times of great hunger, she tells the following story:

> Once, when my father was still alive, he came home from the synagogue and said, "There is a man dying on a bench." He asked my mother to give me a bowl of soup and send me to feed the dying man. This bowl of soup was the children's soup. I went to the synagogue. The man really was dying. I tried to feed him, holding his head with one hand and feeding him with the other. He swallowed slowly but he swallowed, he was very hungry. The next day he died. I was the last person to see him. He told me that he came from Warsaw, he had a family and was very wealthy, and if I could rescue him he would give me everything he had. And he died. When I came home my parents told me, "You did a big *mitsvah.*" From a Jewish religious point of view, maybe I did what I had to do, but believe me I was jealous of every spoonful I fed him, as I wanted to eat it myself. I was very hungry. At this moment I saw the Angel of Death in front of my eyes.

Miriam's father had a long beard but refused to cut it even when she told him that she saw how brutally the Germans forced Jews to cut their beards off in the streets. Later, he allowed her mother to trim it somewhat. He was a big, healthy man before the ghetto, but he had already lost nearly ninety pounds after arriving in the ghetto. Yet on Passover in 1941 he refused to eat because the food was not kosher. Miriam will never forget this "horrible Passover."

In 1942, during the *groyse shpere* (the great curfew), in which her father was taken away, Miriam wrote another poem in Polish, which follows.

Song 20

Lodz Ghetto 1942

Trzy razy księżyc odmienił się złoty
I ja do życia staciłem ochotę.

Maleńką kromkę chleba już zjadłem
Prócz niej kartofel surowy (co skradłem)
Całą rodzinę zabrali mi w szperze
Matka struchlała, ryczała, jak zwierzę,
Nogi Niemca-kata głaskała
O życie dzieci swoich błagała . . .
Więc ją za ramię silnie schwycili
I już jej nie było po jednej chwili.
Przed bramą wóz stał pełny "wybranych"
I na nim mama moja kochana
I ojciec, brodę targając daremnie,
Dwie siostry i brat
Jechali beze mnie.
Jedynym się został na podwórku
Prócz mnie sąsiadki ta chuda córka
I szewc z przeciwka
I głuchy Srul
Nie słyszał krzyków
Nie słyszał kul.
Z całego domu została nas czwórka.
Wnet krzyki doszły z innego podwórka . . .
Trzy razy księżyc odmienił się złoty
I ja do życia straciłem ochotę.
A jeśli stąd wyjdę żywy i cały
Jak to opowiem co tu się działo?
Czy ludzie normalni, wolni, uwierzą
Co tu się działo w tej strasznej szperze?
Czy ktoś uwierzy na całym świecie
Co się przeżyło w łódzkim getcie?

Lodz Ghetto 1942

(Based on the rhythm of a Polish poem by Słowacki)

Three times the moon changed its golden color
And I've lost my will to live.
I've already eaten my small pieces of bread
And the raw potato I stole.
They took away my family during the *shpere:*
Mother cried like an animal
She kissed the German soldier's feet
And begged for the lives of her children.
The German grabbed her:
And, in one minute, she wasn't there anymore.
Before the gate stood a cart full of the "chosen"
And on this cart was my beloved mother.
My father shaved his beard for nothing.

My two sisters and my brother,
They left without me
And left in the backyard there was only myself,
The neighbor's skinny daughter,
The shoemaker from across the street,
And Srul, the deaf man.
He did not hear the shouting
Neither the shooting.
From the entire building, only four were left.
Meanwhile, more screams were coming from another backyard.
Three times the moon changed its golden color
And I've lost my will to live.
If I survive all this in one piece
How could I tell what happened here?
Would free normal people believe
What happened in this horrible *shpere*?
Would anyone in the whole world believe
What happened in the Lodz ghetto?

This poem was based on a poem by the famous Polish writer Juliusz Słowacki. The original poem, "Ojciec Zadżumionych" (The father of the ones who died from the plague), Miriam explains, is known to every Polish youth.

The original poem speaks of an Arab who buried all his family in the desert after they died from the plague. The hero of the poem describes how he buries each child and is finally the only one left alive, like Job. At the end, a talking fruit tree asks him, "Old man, where is your family?" And the Arab thinks, "What shall I answer? What shall I say? I buried all of them, one by one."

Miriam recalls this poem every time she describes her father's deportation. He was the first of her family to be taken during the *groyse shpere*. Her older brother, who was already married and had three children, had already been taken to Auschwitz. Miriam's mother was sick, as were two of her sisters. Did she foresee the deaths of most of her family in 1942? Or did she alter the poem when recreating it in 1945? The metaphor of the Arab in the poem is clear; Miriam, however, was not fortunate enough to bury her family herself.

Miriam often asks herself why *she* survived. Her answer is that she was the "right" age: In Lodz she was young enough to believe that there would be an end to the suffering and was buoyed by the hope. By the time she arrived in Auschwitz, she was old and robust enough in appearance to pass "the selection" and so she was spared.

After enduring these ordeals, she realized that she would be one of the few survivors in her family to tell her story.

She wrote another song in Polish, based on the tune of a Yiddish folksong called "Mayn tate iz a smarovoznik" (My father is a train mechanic), after the first line of its second verse. Cahan (1957:440), in his Yiddish song collection, titles it "Vus bistu ketsele broygez" (Why are you angry, Pussycat?). In 1945, while waiting in Italy for her immigration papers, Miriam translated her poem into Yiddish under the title "Vinter 1942" (Winter 1942).

Song 21

Vinter 1942—Geto Lodz (Winter 1942—Lodz Ghetto)

Verse 1:
Tate mame lign in beys-oylem.
Der brider iz avek geshikt.
Di shvester krank geyt ayngeboygn,
Ikh bin fun hunger tsugedrikt.

Verse 2:
In shtib nishtu kayn lefl esn,
Kayn broyt, kayn meyrl zet men nisht.
Tsu kayen hob ikh shoyn fargesn.
Laydik puste iz der tish.

Verse 3:
S'iz kalt, farfroyrn mayne finger,
Ikh hob nor laptsies oyf di fis,
By nakht ikh veyn fin groysn hinger,
Dos leybn fintster iz un mis.

Verse 4:
Es iz in himl keyn rakhmones,
Der sotn shteyt dort un er lakht,

Fin di yesoymim un almones
In lodzer geto tsugemakht.

Verse 5:
Ikh gay arum zikh vi an alter,
Di oygn zenen nas un royt,
Dos himl fintster iz a kalte,
Un morgn kimen vet der toyt.

Verse 1:
Father and mother in the graveyard.
My brother sent away.
My sister is sick, a walking cripple,
I am weak from hunger.

Verse 2:
In the house there is no food at all,
No bread, not even carrots could we find.
I have already forgotten how to chew.
Empty, vacant is the table.

Verse 3:
It's cold, my fingers are frozen,
I have only slippers on my feet,
At night I cry from my great hunger,
My life is dark and miserable.

Verse 4:
There is no mercy in heaven,
Satan stands there and laughs,
He laughs at the orphans and widows
Locked up in the Lodz ghetto.

Verse 5:
I walk around like an old man,
My eyes are wet and red,
The sky is dark and cold,
And tomorrow death will come.

To be grammatically correct, the words *dos himl* in verse 5 should be *der himl;* however, Miriam sings *dos himl,* apologizing for her "bad" Yiddish. I have therefore represented it just as she sang it. Miriam is also inconsistent in her pronunciation of words, shifting between the Lithuanian way, which she probably learned at a later age, and the way it was pronounced in Lodz. I did not correct this inconsistency.

Miriam used the rhythm and theme of "a story of a Jewish family" in the original folksong to describe the new reality. The original song describes a poor, working-class family in which the father labors at greasing train wheels, the mother steals fish from the market, the brother is a pickpocket, and the sister is crazy. A generation earlier the situation was not any more dignified for the family since the aunt was a prostitute and the uncle was sick and hospitalized. However, in spite of the grandparents' low social status, they hold respected positions at the Jewish religious services in the synagogue and at the ritual bath. The one who speaks in the song is probably the boyfriend of the young sister in this family, who wants to get married. The original song begins:

> Vus bistu, ketsele, broygez?
> Vus geystu aropgelozt di noz?
> Efsher vilstu visn fun dayn sheyne mishpukhe?
> Vel ikh dir zugn, ketsele, ot dos:
>
> Dayn tate iz a smarovoznik,
> Dayn mame ganvet fish in mark,
> Un dayn bruder iz a marevikher,
> Un dayn shvester tra la la la!
>
> Dayn zayde is a shtikl shames,
> Dayn bobe a tukerin in bod,
> Un dayn mume shtayt oyfn ogol,
> Un dayn feter ligt in a shpitol.

> Why are you angry, Pussycat?
> Why are you so sad?
> Would you maybe like to know about your beautiful family?
> I will tell you, pussycat, this:
>
> Your father is a train maintenance mechanic,
> Your mother steals fish from the market,
> And your brother is a pickpocket,
> And your sister, tra la la la! [is crazy]
>
> Your grandfather is a sexton [in a synagogue],
> Your grandmother is a ritual-bath attendant,
> Your aunt is a prostitute,
> Your uncle stays in a hospital.

The original song concerns the situation of the working-class Jews in Czarist Russia. It is a humorous song which calls for amused sympathy. Miriam's contrafact lyrics are not humorous, but speak of deep despair and helplessness.

The irony that emerges when one contrasts the original song with the new lyrics is very powerful: the old tune spoke of a time when people believed that things could be worse; destiny, no matter how harsh, could be greeted with a smile. Miriam's new lyrics, on the other hand, speak to a present of unimaginable horror. The only one smiling in the ghetto is Satan.

Despite the appearance of her personal involvement, Miriam's lyrics do not refer to her own family situation. At the time she wrote them (1942) her mother, sisters, and younger brother were still alive. Thus, the poem perhaps is to be understood on the one hand in a historical sense, a description of commonplace ghetto "disappearances" and dissolutions of families, and on the other, in a prophetic sense—Miriam was indeed to lose her parents and most of her family.

The *groyse shpere* was such a traumatic event that Miriam had to express it in another song, written in 1943, in Polish:

Song 22

Lodz Ghetto, 1943 (I)

Jadą dzieci, jadą drogą,
Siostrzyczka i brat,
I nadziwić się nie mogą
Jaki podły świat.

Tu się widzi żółtą łatę
Tam kolczasty drut
My odziani w stare szmaty
I drewniany but.

Wczoraj wzięli stąd sieroty
I wysłali w dal.
Na płacz zbiera się ochota,
W sercu smutek, żal.

Jadą dzieci, jadą drogą
Dokąd? Dokąd? Gdzie?
Tylko płakać jeszcze mogą
Póki pociąg mknie . . .

Children are going, are going away,
A brother and a sister
Wondering about the world,
What a nasty world.

Here you see a yellow patch,
There you see barbed-wire fence,
We wear worn-out clothes
And wooden shoes.

Yesterday they took away the orphans
And sent them far away,
One wants to cry,
And it is sad, and it's a pity.

Children are going, are going away,
In their last days
They can only cry
As long as the train keeps going.

The original song is a Polish children's song, "Jadą Dzieci, Jadą Drogą" (Children are going, are going away). It speaks of children who wonder about the beauty of the world. Following is an English translation of some lines from the original song:[3]

Children are going, are going away,
A brother and a sister,
Wondering about the world:
What a beautiful world.

Here is hidden a small house
Under a straw roof,
Next to the house a wide-branched tree
And a scarecrow stands in a potato field.

The contrast between an original tune evoking nostalgic moments from a beautiful world, and the new lyrics about imprisoned, innocent children starving in a world full of death, adds to the tragedy described in this song.

Miriam wrote the song after most of the orphan children of the ghetto were removed. These Jewish children were leaving, too, going to an unknown destination where death awaited them. By 1941 Miriam knew that adults and children were being deported from the ghetto, never to return.

As a counselor in Gordonya, Miriam was in charge of a group of thirty children, ages eight to ten. She was seventeen when she began teaching them, conducting the assembly in a field during the summer and leading the groups in debates, lectures, and singing. She remembers that one of the moral issues discussed was: "Is it permissible to lie?" She was deeply touched by the young children's response. One said, "It is forbidden to lie, but if I see a German killing my mother, I will not tell my father about it." Another said, "It is not permitted to lie, but if I can't sleep at night because I am so hungry, and my mother asks me why, I will say I am not hungry so my mother will not cry."

Miriam also recalls vividly another issue they discussed: "Are the Jews as bad as the Germans tell us?" The children had no satisfactory answer for that. Later Miriam found out that all of them were shipped off in a single deportation of orphan children in 1942. Miriam dedicated this song to these children, remembering their dark, questioning eyes.

In 1943 she also wrote another piece based on a Polish folksong, "Stokrotka Rosła Polna" (Flowers are blooming in the fields):

Song 23

Lodz Ghetto, 1943 (II)

Tu w getcie koło mostu,
Niemiecki żolnierz trwa,
On sterczy tam poprostu,
A na nim kroczę ja.[7]

On trzyma strzelbę w ręku
I patrzy na mnie się,
Me serce pełne lęku,
I płakać mi się chce.

Ja chodzić już nie mogę
Bo głod zabija mnie,
Bezsilne moje nogi
I ręce trzęsą się.

Może go piorun trzaśnie,
Cholera weźmie w mig,
A ja na moscie właśnie,
Usłyszę jego krzyk.

Czy ktoś Niemców ukaże?
Kto z getta zwolni nas!
Na moście stoję, marzę
Że przyjdzie taki czas.

Here in the ghetto,
Next to the bridge,
A German soldier stands,
As I cross the bridge.

He's holding a gun in his hand,
And he looks at me,
I am afraid
And I want to cry.

I can't walk any more
Because I am dying of hunger,
My legs are paralyzed
And my hands are shaking.

Maybe he will be struck by lightning,
Maybe the cholera will take him,
And I, on the bridge,
Will hear his screaming.

If someone would punish the Germans
And rescue us from the ghetto!
On the bridge I stand and dream
That this day will come.

This song expresses Miriam's anger and call for vengeance. She stands on one of the three bridges of the ghetto, those symbols of survival. While crossing the bridge one time meant successfully reaching the workplace, crossing twice was just as significant—one had returned from work. Working in the ghetto, being productive, meant surviving (cf. street song no. 18). Crossing the crowded bridges was not easy, however, since each was guarded by German soldiers. People were frequently kidnapped or even killed on these bridges.

Anger and a call for revenge can be perceived not only in Miriam's poems but in poetry written in many of the ghettos and camps during this period. Her hope for a better future vanished after the *groyse shpere,* in which she lost many friends and family members, and her own suffering increased as time went on; when action was impossible only anger remained.[4]

The original Polish folksong was about the beauties of life, which only adds to the sense of loss in Miriam's lyrics; she writes of the loss of joy, beauty, and a free life.

Miriam's next song was composed toward the end of her ghetto period, in late 1944. It is based on a Polish folksong, "Za Górami, Za Lasami, Tańcowała Małgorzatkaz Żołnierzami . . . (Behind the mountains and the forest, Margozatka danced with soldiers), and was written originally in Polish. This poem, again, speaks of the poet's despair:

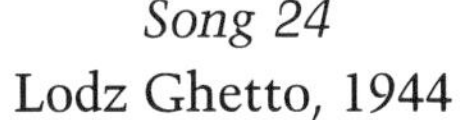

Song 24

Lodz Ghetto, 1944

Za kolczastym, silnym drutem,
Łódzkie getto, łódzkie getto, jest zakute.[8]

Naokoło Niemcy wszędzie
Stąd uciekać, stąd uciekać nikt nie będzie.

W getcie dzielą, zupy garnek,
I do tego sacharyny kilka ziarnek.

Może dadzą rzodkiew zgniłą,
By się w getcie, by się w getcie jakoś żyło.

Wczoraj odszedł transport duży,
Nic dobrego, nic dobrego to nie wróży.

Poszedł ojciec, poszła matka,
Sam zostałem, sam zostałem do ostatka.

Za drutami, za drutami,
Wszyscy będziem, wszyscy będziem pochowani.

Behind a strong barbed-wire fence,
Lodz Ghetto, Lodz Ghetto is sealed.

Surrounded by Germans everywhere,
Nobody can escape from here.

In the ghetto they portion out a pot of soup,
And in addition, some crumbs of saccharine.

Maybe they will give us rotten radishes,
So in the ghetto, in the ghetto we shall live somehow.

Yesterday, a big transport was sent,
It brings nothing good, nothing good.

Father went, mother went,
I stayed behind alone, I will remain alone, until the end.

Behind a barbed-wire fence
We shall all be buried.

Miriam learned this song before the war from her family's Polish housekeeper. The original song tells of a girl who goes dancing with some soldiers; her parents show up at the dance and ask her to come home. The girl tells them: "I do not want to go home. I want to dance with the soldiers." Again, the juxtaposition of the new lyrics with a tune that evokes more pleasant, prewar times contributes to the sense of loss.

Later the same year, Miriam felt the need to express the destiny of the Jewish people in the ghetto. She wrote about their lives as prisoners, lacking freedom, food, and hope, everything except the primitive instinct to survive. She wrote the song after her girlfriend Henyah was taken in a transport. She imagined that if they took Henyah, she could be next.

Times were growing worse in the ghetto—no family was left intact. The young prisoners like Miriam were obligated to work in the ghetto workshops as well as at home. At this time, young people from different organizations met very rarely since they were absorbed in their own problems. As Miriam describes it, "At the beginning we used to meet, sing, dance, study at our youth organization meetings. We did not hear the screaming of people whose loved ones were deported, we did not see the funerals of the others. Life looked normal! Later, after 1940 and more so after 1942, we all sank into this abnormal reality of the ghetto."

After the deep depression of her 1944 song comes the only one expressing hope. Miriam's last ghetto song is titled "Kalt" (Cold). It was indeed composed in retrospect, after her deportation to Italy in 1945, and was the only song she originally wrote in Yiddish.

Song 25

Kalt: A lidl fin lodzger getto, 1945
(Cold: A Song from the Lodz Ghetto, 1945)

Verse 1:
Kalt.
In groyzam ligt der vinter nakht.
Ikh gey zikh aynsam un fertrakht,
Dos himl fil mit vulken tribe.

Verse 2:
Kalt.
Der kalter vint hot zikh tsulakht,
Es reygnt shoyn di gantse nakht.
Mayn harts geyt oys tsu dir mayn libe.

Refren:
S'gibt aza velt,
Vi mentshn tantsn oyf gelt,
Vi es gist zikh purpur vayn,

In gold, in zilber shayn,
S'gibt aza velt . . .

Verse 3:
Kalt.
Vi groyzam iz mayn tifer shrek,
Ven du fin mir bist shoyn avek
Aleyn bin ikh dokh du geblibn.

Verse 4:
Kalt.
Ikh zey vagonen tsugemakht
Zey forn shnel di gantse nakht.
Vi hot men dikh avek getribn?

Refren:
S'gibt aza velt . . .

Verse 5:
Kalt.
Es falt a shney du oyf di gas,
Farfroyrn, finster iz in nas.
Vi troyerik s'iz di neshome.

Verse 6:
Kalt.
Tsu vet dokh kumen aza tsayt?
Un efsher iz er nisht gants vayt?
Mir veln nemen a nekume!

Refren:
S'gibt aza velt . . .

Verse 1:
Cold.
How ruthless is the winter night.
I walk alone, deep in thought,
The sky is full of dreary clouds.

Verse 2:
Cold.
The chilly wind begins to laugh,
It will rain all night.
My heart goes out to you, my love.

Refrain:
This is such a world,
Where people dance on money,
And purple wine is being poured,
In gold and silver goblets,
This is such a world . . .

Verse 3:
Cold.
How ruthless is my deep despair,
When you went away from me
I was left here alone.

Verse 4:
Cold.
I see closed railroad cars
Speeding by all through the night.
Where did they take you?

Refrain:
This is such a world . . .

Verse 5:
Cold.
Snow is falling in the street,
It is freezing, dark and wet.
How sad is my soul.

Verse 6:
Cold.
Will the time ever come?
Perhaps it will come soon?
We shall live to take revenge!

Refrain:
This is such a world . . .

In this song Miriam is using motifs similar to those in her earlier Yiddish song, "Vinter 1942" (Winter 1942). Both speak of the winter, of cold and darkness outside and in the ghetto. This song, however, has some hope in it and calls for vengeance.

She remembered that the inspiration for the first verse and refrain came from a song her mother used to sing. Miriam adapted the original song, composing two additional verses. Khane Mlotek claims that the melody comes from a Yiddish lullaby titled "Vigndik a krank kind" (Soothing a sick child).[5] Miriam used the song's mood to express her recent experiences: "Because it had a sweet melody, I decided to write it. I felt people would like it. The *shliḥim* [Israeli emissaries], who took care of us, encouraged us to write so we would not forget."[6]

After Miriam sang this song for me, she paused, then said in emotionally choked tones, "This is what I felt."

Before I thanked her for the interview and turned off my tape recorder she broke into tears. "For heaven's sake," she asked me, "why did we not become crazy? God, why did these people not go mad? Why did they not kill each other in the ghetto? Why did they survive? Today I cannot understand it."

Summary

In the ghetto, Miriam Harel expressed herself in the language she knew best, Polish. Her feelings had to be conveyed, and words became her weapon. Obsessed with hunger, she described it in various ways in six poems and songs out of the seven she has written. Unlike many of the ghetto inhabitants, she realized that adults and children were being removed and sent to their deaths; this found expression in nearly all her songs. Singing for her family in a domestic context set her free to express her feelings; no official censorship or unofficial "audience requirements" influenced her themes. Unlike the street performers, who sang for a mass audience, Miriam could sing about helplessness and the lack of hope.

She could also express her wish for vengeance in her own way. Although the themes of hunger, death, and the call for revenge are found in the street songs as well, Miriam's feelings of hopelessness and her descriptions of the mass deportations have no equivalent in other genres. Miriam's repertoire stems from four years' experience in the ghetto (1940 to 1944), whereas most of the street songs were composed during the first two years, when times were different and hope still prevailed.

Since Miriam could recall the sources of her melodies, one can accurately identify her parody technique. Evocation of the original melody clearly added to the message of Miriam's own texts. She was aware of this, and such was her intent.

Miriam Harel used her multilingualism intentionally in her compositions, in choosing both the language for the text and the source of the music. Her artistic action involved creativity and selective esthetic response, and it communicated her mood and thoughts, then and now.

NOTES

1. I conducted all interviews with Miriam Harel in Hebrew in August 1983, August 1985, and August 1986; and I recorded and transcribed them.

2. All songs in Polish are according to Miriam's book. She published her memoirs after the completion of my original research, in a book entitled *A'khshav Kvar Mutar Livkot* (Now you may cry) (Tel Aviv 1989). She

included her Polish poems in their original language along with her own Hebrew translation.

3. This version of the original song was recorded from my mother, Esther Flam (b. 1926, Zbydniow, Poland), who also assisted me in the translations from Polish to Hebrew. Chava Rosenfarb quotes another paraphrased version based on the same Polish children's song which inspired another ghetto inhabitant to write about the destiny of the Jewish children.

4. Kübler-Ross describes six stages in which terminally ill people react to the knowledge of their fate. The stages as schematized by Kübler-Ross are: denial and isolation, anger, bargaining, depression and acceptance. Throughout these stages (which last for different periods of time), hope persists. In Miriam's poetry I found parallels to three categories: anger, depression, and hope. Since the comparison of the Holocaust victims with terminally ill patients is an apt one, I feel it not inappropriate to categorize her songs according to this framework.

5. Khane Mlotek, the well-known expert in Yiddish songs, conveyed this opinion in a letter to me, September 1989.

6. The emissaries were sent by the Jewish Agency to care for displaced persons (like Miriam) and to arrange their *aliyah* (immigration) to Palestine.

7. The last two lines of each verse in this song are sung twice.

8. The last line of each verse in this song is sung twice.

5

Other Contexts for Singing: The Theater, the Youth Organization, and the Workplace

Through Yaakov Rotenberg we can understand the context of street performance, and through Miriam Harel that of domestic entertainment. Yet they also recall songs that, though sung in the ghetto, were not composed there. This chapter presents a variety of other song styles, defined as genres according to their context of performance.

Pinchas Shaar (Schwartz) will introduce us to the ghetto theater. Born in Lodz in 1920, he now resides in New York City, making his living as an artist: "I can't do anything else, so I paint."[1] Pinchas has been painting since he was five years old and served in the ghetto as the "official" theater painter and set decorator.

The Theater

Pinchas's Story

Pinchas, it seemed, did not really want to be interviewed. His answers to my questions were as brief as could be. He was not convinced that I had chosen the right man to interview. Although he speaks fluent Yiddish, Polish, French, and English, he preferred to converse with me in Hebrew as a sign of respect for my native language.

In the living room of his Manhattan apartment, surrounded by his books and original works of art, he opened the conversation by asking, "Why are you interested in me?" I explained that I was interested in survivors who were sensitive to art and who took part in artistic productions in the Lodz ghetto. He then admitted that he had not only seen all the theater shows, but that he had created their set decorations and participated in the artistic committees.

He became annoyed when I asked him, "What happened in 1942 when the theater was closed down?" He responded:

> For you, the theater is a central issue. But in real life, the theater was a side issue. Most of the people in the ghetto did not even know it existed. Like today, you will find people who are not interested in theater. Ask some people what's going on on Broadway tonight and they would not know. Because only a certain type of person is interested in theater. In the ghetto, some people attended the theater in an organized way, as they received tickets through their working places. For them it was an unexpected entertainment. But not everyone got tickets. So, asking what happened in the ghetto when the theater was closed down is like asking what will happen in New York City if I drop the cup of tea that I am drinking now. When they closed down the theater, it had no impact whatsoever on the life in the ghetto.

Although he enjoyed his work for the ghetto theater, Pinchas never considered artistic work a means of survival. He could not earn a living from his set designs since all theater work was voluntary, unpaid. His talented hands could not support him financially, but they helped him get through otherwise.

Describing his time in the ghetto, Pinchas remarked: "At the beginning there was a severe danger of typhus, so they took me to work for the health department drafting signposts illustrating how to fight the disease. I worked there for about three months. Then they organized the statistics department. I was the first one to work there under the supervision of Neftalin.[2] In this department I did the graphics for the ghetto's money, and other jobs. I was starving in this department, I was swollen from hunger. I stayed there until 1942."

It is not surprising that Pinchas's attitude toward art was ambivalent. He was talented, but his talent would not sustain him during the abnormal times of the ghetto. I asked him to continue his story, which even he admits is rather interesting: "I had a friend in school who was the son of Rumkowski's sister-in-law. He left Lodz in 1939, before the war. This woman used to be seen with Rumkowski on public occasions, since Rumkowski did not have a wife. [This was before Rumkowski's ghetto marriage on 27 December 1941; see Dobroszycki 1984 : 101.] She was called 'the princess from Kent,' *ver hot zi gekent und ver vil zi kenen.*" He explained the joke:

> Who knew her before, and who will know her after the war? Before the war I helped her son to draw the diagrams and drawings he needed for his studies in chemistry, physics, etc. So I used to come to their house. But I did not think she would remember me. One day I was walking in the ghetto's streets and she passed by, riding her *droshka* [cart]; she

> recognized me. She said: "Pinek"—that's how they used to call me—"you look terrible. Call me in a day or two, and I will find a better job for you." Next day, I was sitting in the statistics department office, and I was called to the phone. With great respect, my fellow workers told me: "Mrs. Rumkowski is asking for you over the phone." And she told me that she'd gotten me a job in the food provisions department [Polish: *prowizacea*] of the bakery. I got that job and held it for almost one year. This saved not only me, but my whole family. I was there until 1943. Then I got even a more important job.

He started to tell me another story, but stopped suddenly, asking himself, "How should I begin?" Finally he found a way and opened with a question: "You know that the liquidation of the ghetto was done in parts? First they took the sick people, then the elderly, then single people. Before that, infants and children. I do not remember dates."

After this preamble he got around to the point of his story:

> Many children were hidden. But in order to survive they had to go to work, and they were spread out over all the *Ressorts* [a ghetto slang word for the workshops]. It created a problem, because when the Germans came to inspect the workshops they could discover the children. The German head of the ghetto, Biebow, was interested in the ghetto's productiveness—he made a lot of money out of it. He would therefore invite German delegations up to the ghetto to show them the products the Jewish population made for them. So someone had a brilliant idea to create a central exhibit place where all the *Ressorts* would show off their products, and the German delegation would not have to inspect the whole ghetto. To create this place was my job. They gave a special house for that. I built showcases like you see nowadays in fashion and jewelry stores. All the time I had the feeling that the Germans would not let us out of the ghetto alive. I did not know yet about the gas chambers, but I was afraid that they would bomb us when they had no longer any need for us. So I decided to build a bunker. And how do you build a bunker? When you take dirt out it piles up. . . . The fact that we were building [the exhibition hall] there helped me to build this bunker without anyone discovering it. We built this bunker over a year and a half, all three brothers. And this bunker saved us.

Pinchas did not want to continue this story in detail, assuming that I had already heard it from his brother, whom I had interviewed earlier. He simply stated that he and his family hid in the bunker until they ran out of food. During the final days of the ghetto the authorities were searching for people to maintain it after the mass deportations of 1944. So the family worked in the ghetto and were finally taken off to a concentration camp. Pinchas noted, "But it was not like Auschwitz, and there we survived and were liberated in Germany" (see Dobroszycki 1984: lxvi n. 168).

This, in brief, is Pinchas's story. The Holocaust does not figure as a theme in his art, but it is an undeniable part of his life experience. His ghetto art remains in the albums he illustrated for the ghetto's statistics department, and is stored in the archives of the YIVO Institute in New York. He has no words to define his painting style; he does not like to talk about it. His paintings, he feels, speak for him better than his words can.

Pinchas describes the nature of the Revue Theater:

> It was a revue, containing ten to fifteen numbers. Eighty percent of the repertoire was prewar pieces which the theater director, Pulaver, remembered from his previous activity in the Ararat Theater. I did not know the pieces from before the war, so my set decorations had to be new. The texts and the music were from before the war. There were also two or three new sketches on ghetto life, topicals. From time to time maybe they also had new musical pieces. The theater was not political, Yankele [Hershkowitz's] songs were much more political. The theater was more abstract, it was concerned with Yiddish literature, poetry, and Jewish folklore.

Pinchas did not feel like singing when I interviewed him. However, he commented on some theater songs I had recorded from other survivors. Most of the theatrical revue repertoire consisted of songs which could be adapted to the new situation: songs about hunger and oppression (part of Jewish life before World War II), and the "universal" song types, lullabies and love songs.

Song 26

Ver der ershter vet lakhn? (Who Will Laugh First?)

Text and music Mordechai Gebirtig

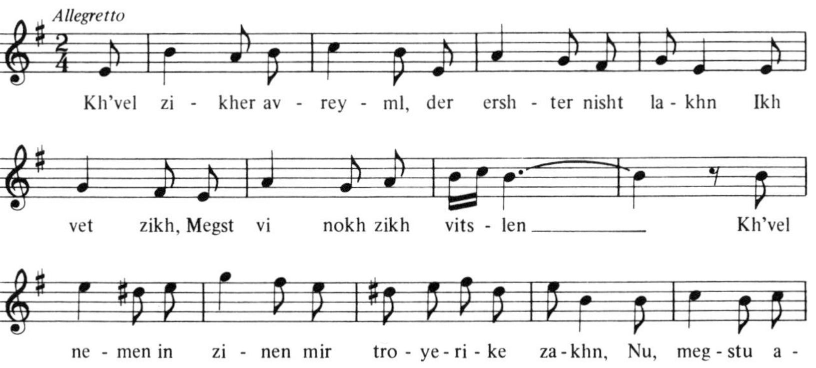

Verse:
Kh'vel zikher, avreyml,
Der ershter nisht lakhn
Ikh vet zikh,
Megst vi nokh zikh vitslen,
Kh'vel nemen in zinen
Mir troyerike zakhn,
Nu, megstu afile mikh kitslen.

Refren:
Vest lakhn, ikh vet zikh,
Vest shloymele, shoyn lakhn
Ikh hob a mitl gor,
A voyle zakh—
Megst hobn zikh in zinen
Di troyerikste zakhn,
Vet muzn zayn bay dir der
Ershter lakh . . .

Letster Refren:
Vest lakhn, vest lakhn,
Aher gib shoyn dos knepl,

Zeh, shloymele,
Vos hob ikh do far dir!
A zemele mit piter,
In heyring a fayn kepl,
Anu, zog shlomke,
Ver vet lakhn friyer?
—A zemele mit piter
Un hering a fayn kepl,
Kh'vel morgn vider
Vetn zikh mit dir.

Verse:
You, Avreyml, definitely
Won't be the first to laugh
I'll bet,
You can make jokes,
But I have in mind
Tragic things,
You can even tickle me.

Refrain:
You will laugh, I'll bet,
You, Shloymele, will laugh,
I will find the way,
A good way—
You could think
Of the most tragic things,
But you will have to crack
The first laugh . . .

Last Refrain:
You will laugh, you will laugh,
Hand me the button,
Look, Shloymele,
What I've got for you!
A roll with butter,
And a fine head of herring,
So, what do you say, Shlomke,
Who will laugh first?
—A roll with butter
And a fine head of herring,
I will once more tomorrow
Bet with you.

This song, which is presented only in part, is a duet composed by Mordechai Gebirtig (1877–1942), a popular Yiddish songwriter before the war who continued to write and compose in the Cracow ghetto.[3]

The song is a duet sung by two boys, Avreyml and Shloymele, who make a bet as to who can make the other laugh first. Shloymele asks: "How can I laugh when my father is sick and cannot find a job? How can I laugh when I am so hungry that the Rabbi hits me for not listening?" Avreymele tries to make him laugh by imitating the sounds of a cat and a dog. At last he shows the contents of his pocket: "A zemele mit piter" (A roll with butter), "In heyring a fayn kepl" (And a fine head of herring), and Shloymele starts to laugh.

Gebirtig probably never had a more perfect empathy with his audience—with the misery and the joy of two boys looking at a roll with butter and a herring head—than with the audience of the ghetto.

The song became a "hit of the ghetto theater" since it suited the new situation so well. With the exception of Pinchas Shaar, who knew that it was a song sung before the war and adapted to the ghetto theater, all of my informants believed the song to be an original ghetto composition. Indeed, most of the interviewees remembered with amusement the song on "A zemele mit piter."[4]

Song 27

A toyber hot gehert (A Deaf Man Heard)

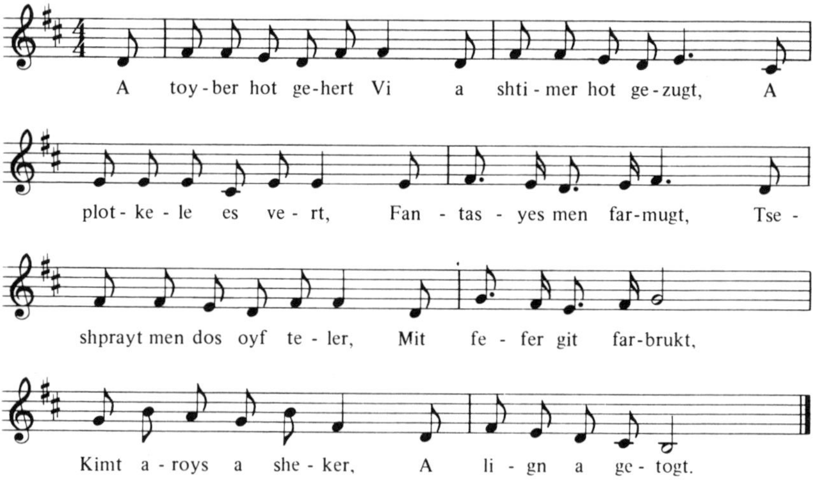

A toy - ber hot ge-hert Vi a shti - mer hot ge - zugt, A

plot - ke - le es ve - rt, Fan - tas - yes men far-mugt, Tse -

shprayt men dos oyf te - ler, Mit fe - fer git far-brukt,

Kimt a - roys a she - ker, A li - gn a ge - togt.

A toyber hot gehert
Vi a shtimer hot gezugt,
A plotkele es vert,
Fantasyes men farmugt,

Tseshprayt men dos oyf teler,
Mit fefer git farbrukt,
Kimt aroys a sheker,
A lign a getogt.

A deaf man heard
What a dumb man said,
A rumor of a plot,
Feeds our fantasies,
Served up on fancy plates,
Spiced so very nice,
Makes a tasty lie,
A beautiful calculated lie.

This verse was sung to me by both Yaakov Rotenberg and Itka Slodowsky. However, they could not say for certain whether they first heard it sung in the streets or in the theater. Yeḥiel Frenkiel confirmed that the song had its origins in a theatrical sketch, where it was followed by another number, "I Am a Little 'Intellectual'" (see song 28, below).

The song "A toyber hot gehert" describes the process of inventing and spreading rumors in the ghetto. The one who hears a rumor is deaf, and the one who spreads it is dumb; as a result a new story is created, a fine story to feed the ghetto's need for fantasy. Indeed, besides fantasy, what was left? Rumkowski, the official source of information, permitted only the news he wanted known to circulate. Thus, rumors served as the most important discovery about present and future events. As Yosef Mulaz, who also recalled the song, described: "Every sentence you'd hear in the ghetto began with 'Have you heard what he was saying?'"[5] Even the *Chronicle* devoted a column to what "People Are Saying." For officials, too, rumors were the main source of information in the ghetto.

Song 28

Ikh bin an inteligentl (I Am an "Intellectual")

Verse 1:
Ikh bin an inteligentl,
Ikh es nisht mit dem hentl,
Oyb ir vilt a dokumentl,
Tsayg ikh aykh dos bald.
Ikh fil mikh do *posvoysku,*
Ikh es kokletn *koynske,*
Bagosn mit *koloyske,*
In ikh shray gevalt!
(oder: In ikh zing mir tsu.)

Refren:
Oy, halt mir s'tepl!
S'tepl halt mir!
In di kartofl,
Oykh bashmalts mir!
Vus toyg mir glikn,
In di rayes shtipn,
Vus toyg mir zupn,
O! zup, zup!

Verse 2:
Es tsit mikh shoyn shtark baym mugn,
Di fis viln mir nisht trugn,
Az es hengt a ratsie in di rayn
Dan ver ikh shoyn gesind.

Di zup is haynt mit knokhn,
S'iz yom tov in der vokhns.
Men tut arayn ale tsores brekhn
In men zingt azoy:

Refren:
Halt mir s'tepl . . .

Verse 1:
I'm an intellectual,
I won't eat with my hand,
But if you want to see a document,
I'll show you right away.
I feel right at home here,
Eating my horseflesh meatballs,
Smothered with cologne,
And yet I scream *gevalt*!
(or: And I sing along.)

Refrain:
Oy, hold my bowl!
Hold my bowl!
As for the potatoes,
Spread them all over!
What luck I got,
Getting shoved in the lines,
What soup I got,
Oh! soup, soup!

Verse 2:
My stomach is in agony,
My feet will carry me no more,
But if there's a food ration waiting
Then I'm soon myself again.
Today we have bone soup,
We'll have our holiday this week.
So put all our troubles away,
And we sing just so:

Refrain:
Hold my bowl . . .[6]

Both Yaakov Rotenberg and Itka Slodowsky recall this song being performed in the Revue Theater. Yeḥiel Frenkiel, when recalling a slightly different version, confirmed it might have been included in one of the topical sketches.

The song describes the destiny of the "little intellectual," referring to the fate of every Jew in the ghetto, who daily faced pushing

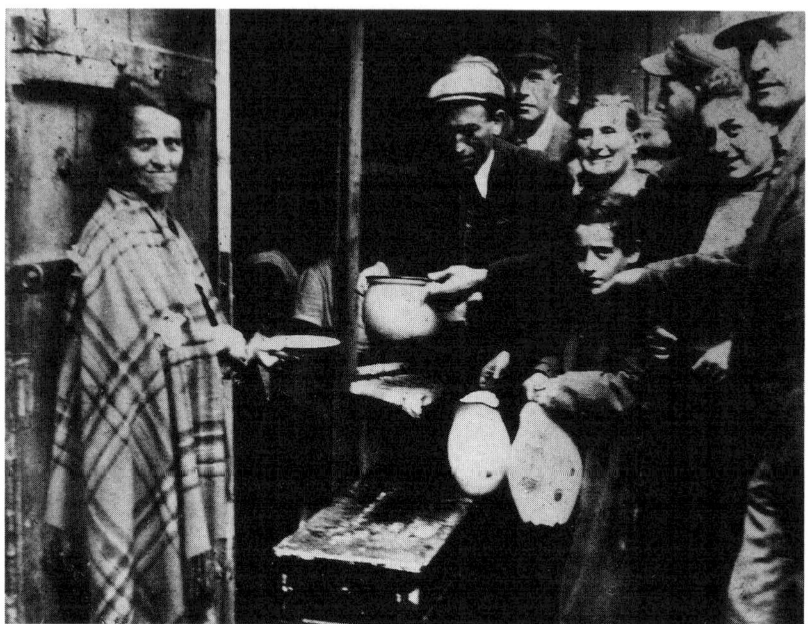

Ghetto inhabitants at the soup kitchen. Zonabend Collection, YIVO Institute for Jewish Research.

and shoving in long lines for the necessities of life. The song uses subtle irony and humor.

The term *inteligentl* (intellectual), perhaps better translated as the more colloquial "smartypants," is ripe with disparaging (or in this case self-disparaging) connotations. Better-educated, upper-class, or merely "fussy" types were commonly labeled with this designation, which thus served as a means of fixing the hierarchy within the ghetto.

The second verse conjures up a very realistic description of hunger on one hand, and lousy food on the other. Accordingly, when the soup is made of bare bones, it becomes a cause for celebration and singing.

Song 29

Tsip tsipele (Tsip Tsipele)

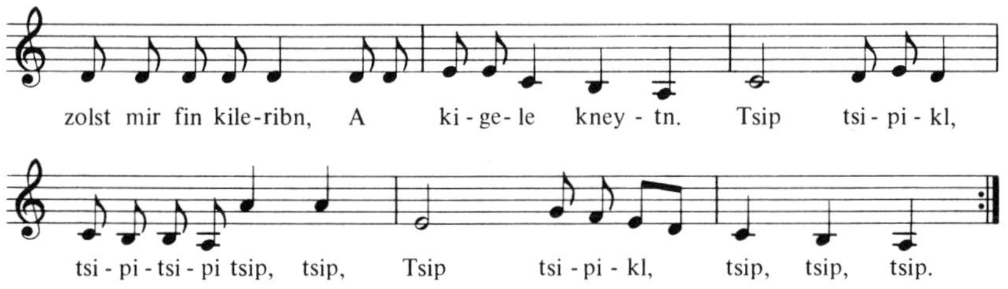

Verse 1:
Oy tsipele mayn vaybele,
Ikh vil dikh epes beytn,
Di zolst mir fin kileribn,
A kigele kneytn.

Refren:
Tsip, tsipikl tsipi, tsipi, tsip . . .
Tsip, tsipikl tsip, tsip, tsip . . .

Verse 2:
Ikh hob genimen a kartofl
Un azoy lang geribn
Biz es iz fin ir nebekh
Gurnisht geblibn.

Refren:
Tsip, tsipikl . . .
Tsip, tsipikl . . .

Verse 3:
Pani vidzelatske:
Ikh mayn nisht kayn gelekhter—
Abisele tifer,
Abisele gedekhter.

Refren:
Tsip, tsipikl . . .
Tsip, tsipikl . . .

Verse 4:
Pani vidzelatske:
Bist grob vi a baleye,
Der prezes vet kimen
Vest di gayn tsi facalye.

Refren:
Tsip, tsipikl . . .

Verse 5:
Pani vidzelatske:
Far ayl in far flokn

Host di dikh gekoyft
A por zaydene zokn.

Refren:
Tsip, tsipikl . . .

Verse 6:
Pani vidzelatske:
Host geganvet burekes,
Der prezes vet kimen
Vest du geyn tsi rozburkes!

Refren:
Tsip, tsipikl . . .

Verse 1:
Oy Tsipele my wife,
I want to ask for something,
Please make for me from kohlrabi,
A tasty pie.

Refrain:
Tsip, tsipikl . . .
Tsip, tsipikl . . .

Verse 2:
I took a nice potato
And grated it so long
Until, unfortunately,
The whole thing disappeared.

Refrain:
Tsip, tsipikl . . .
Tsip, tsipikl . . .

Verse 3:
Madam Wydzielaczka:
I don't mean to make a joke—
Dip a little dipper,
A little thicker.

Refrain:
Tsip, tsipikl . . .
Tsip, tsipikl . . .

Verse 4:
Madam Wydzielaczka:
You're fat like a washtub,
When the President gets here
He'll make you a gutter-sweeper.

Refrain:
Tsip, tsipikl . . .

Verse 5:
Madam Wydzielaczka:
For oil and for oatmeal
You bought yourself
A pair of silk stockings.

Refrain:
Tsip, tsipikl . . .

Verse 6:
Madam Wydzielaczka:
You've stolen some beets,
When the President gets here
He'll make you a building wrecker!

Refrain:
Tsip, tsipikl . . .

The song was sung by Itka Slodowsky and by Yeḥiel Frenkiel; parts of it are quoted in Rosenfarb's trilogy (1972, 3:23 and 76). Itka and Yeḥiel remembered it as part of the repertoire of the Revue Theater. "Tsip," or "Tsipi," or "Tsipikl" is the affectionate diminutive for Tsipora (literally and onomatopoetically, "bird"). It refers to an earlier song titled "Tsig tsigetsapl" by taking the first syllable of the word *tsig* [Yidd.: goat] and its nonsense variations.

This song is related to the *kuplet,* a comedic genre frequently encountered in the Yiddish musical theater (see Sandrow 1977:422 in Werb 1987:64). In this style, performers would "improvise" additional lyrics within a given theater song in order to insert humorous topical references. The *kuplet* can be traced to the Yiddish *badkhonim,* entertainers who excelled in improvising topical verses at Jewish weddings and other occasions. The original *kuplet* titled "Tsig tsigetsapl" (Goat, little goat) is a humorous song about a goat which the Rabbi ordered to be brought to the ritual bath. The goat escaped, was caught, and then the Rabbi realized that the goat embodied an evil spirit. He ordered his followers to recite the *ha'gomel.* The song ends with admiration for the believers and a curse to the skeptical (Vinkovetzky 1985, 3:65–68).

The first and second verses depict the ghetto's food fantasies, with the singer's wife preparing a feast from the very humble ingredients available.

The third verse introduces a real individual, Pani Wydzielaczka, the soup server. The soup kitchens were established by Rumkowski to supply soup to the ghetto inhabitants. Obviously, those close to the pot got more to eat. The hungry others could only wait—and hope that someday Pani Wydzielaczka would be caught and punished for her many thefts. And as creative as the cook and the soup server must be to "get by" or "get away" with her thieving, so, too, could be Rumkowski, if he caught her.

The woman, Pani Wydzielaczka, fat, healthy, and well dressed, is entreated to dig her ladle deep so that something substantial might fall into the bowl of the lucky person. It should be noted that the Polish honorific "Pani" (Madam) is given sarcastically to the Jewish soup-server. No Polish women were employed in the ghetto.

Another source for this song cites a sarcastic version of this verse in which Pani Wydzielaczka answers the request and sings:

Ven kh'volt gehat,
Zol ekh azoy lebn,
Vi kh'vol enk ale gern gegebn!

If I had,
I swear to God,
I would willingly give you all!

Hunger, corruption, and hope for "judgment" are described in this theatrical ghetto *kuplet.* This is the only remnant of the *badkhonim* tradition in a theater form known to me from the ghetto repertoire.

Song 30

Ver klapt dos azoy shpet bay nakht?
(Who Knocks Here So Late at Night?)

(Sie:)
Ver klapt du azoy shpet bay nakht?

(Er:)
Es klapt der geto hinger.
Efn, efn a provizatsyele,
Vet mir vern gringer.

(Sie:)
Vi ken ikh dir efenen?
Kh'hob moyre far dem altn.

(Er:)
Efn, efn a provizatsyele,
Ikh vel es git bahaltn.

(Sie:)
Ver klapt du shpet bay nakht?

(Er:)
Es klapt di geto laydn,
Dray yur in geto,
Yetst miz men zikh tseshaydn.

(She:)
Who knocks out here so late at night?

(He:)
It is the ghetto's hunger.
Open, open the provision store,
That will make it easier.

(She:)
How can I open up that store?
For I fear "the Elder."

(He:)
Open, open the provision store,
I will hide it well.

(She:)
Who knocks out here so late at night?

(He:)
It is the ghetto's suffering,
Three years in the ghetto,
Now comes the time that we must part.

This song is a ghetto version of a Yiddish folksong of the same title included in several published collections (Cahan 1957:104–5; Beregovski 1982:327; Vinkovetzky 1983, 1:49–50).[7] All these versions are textually similar. In Beregovski, it is a love song concerning a young man, Berele Kabantshik, and his beloved Brayndele. Berele asks Brayndele to open the door for him so that he might come in and visit her. However, she is afraid of being discovered by (in successive verses) her mother, father, brother, and sister, and sings: "Ikh hob moyre" (I am afraid of . . .), and all the implorings of Berele are in vain; her "entrance" remains "intact."

This song is perhaps the most "Freudian" of the ghetto repertoire. In it, the folksong's human cast is transformed into raw symbols of "lust" (hunger) and the source of frustration (the off-limits storehouse). The basic animal yearning for sex, transformed by social custom in the original, becomes the even more basic desire for food—aggravated by bureaucratic red tape and corruption. Interestingly, the maiden's over-protective family has been replaced in the ghetto by "Der Alte" Rumkowski.

My primary source for this song was a home recording made by Max Nurenberg (1892–1979) about ten years ago. Nurenberg wished the recording to be a remembrance for his family, and they passed it on to Cantor Samuel Kelemer of Los Angeles, who gave it to me. Among other items, Nurenberg sings a medley of three ghetto songs in Yiddish, the first being "Ver klapt dos azoy shpet bay nakht." Since I was not able to interview the singer, I cannot present details about when and how he learned his songs; however, their significance to his life is manifest in the fact that he chose to make them, in a sense, his testament.

Despair and helplessness are the underpinnings of "Ver klapt dos azoy shpet bay nakht." After "three years in the ghetto" the only desire is to escape, to be free again. Indeed, in the other two songs Max Nurenberg includes in his ghetto medley, he expresses the dream of escape, of beginning a new life. The second song opens with the lines:

Ikh fur avek shoyn,
Ikh fur fin geto;
Di geyle late
Iz mayne tiketo.

I am already going away,
Going away from the ghetto;
The Yellow Badge
Is my ticket.

The final song expresses hope for the future:

A biner vayter (x3)
Vet shoyn vern git,
A biner vayter,
Zing zhe mit mir mit!

On the next stage (x3)
It will be good,
On the next stage,
So let us sing together!

Again, my uncle, Yaakov Flam, provides a variant of the song, closer in spirit to the original folksong than Nurenberg's grim version. (See also the version quoted by Rosenfarb [1972, 2:348].) Yaakov Flam's version is as follows:

Ver klapt dos azoy shpet bay nakht?
(Who Knocks Here So Late at Night?)

[Sie:]
Ver klapt dos azoy shpet bay nakht?

[Er:]
Yankele bulantchik,
Efn, efn, brontchele,
Ikh bin dokh dayn kokhantchik.

[Sie:]
Vi ken ikh dir efenen?
Kh'hob moyre far dem altn.

[Er:]
Efn, efn, brontchele,
M'vet zekh bayde bahaltn.

[Sie:]
Vi ken ikh dir efenen?
Kh'bob moyre far dem tatn.

[Er:]
Efn, efn, brontchele,
M'vet makhn a git mismatn.

[She:]
Who knocks so late at night?

[He:]
Yankele Bulantchik,

Open, open, Brontchele,
I am your beloved.

[She:]
How can I open the door?
For I fear "the Eldest."

[He:]
Open, open, Brontchele,
We both will hide there.

[She:]
How can I open the door?
For I fear "the father."

[He:]
Open, open, Brontchele,
We will steal together.

For Flam, the song retained the resonance of a lovesong. He smiled as he elaborated on certain of its obscure points: "You see, Yankele Bulantchik wants to get to the *prowizacea,* that's where they keep the food. And he wants his beauty Brontchele to help him get there." Flam's version is unquestionably less Freudian in its implications than Nurenberg's; however, he cautioned me that the word *mismatn* (a Polish-Yiddish slang term for "stealing") is a naughty word.

Song 31

Makh tsi di eygelekh (Close Your Little Eyes)

Text: Isaiah Shpigl (1906–1990)

Music: David Beyglman (1887–1944)

Makh tsi di eygelekh,
Ot kimen feygelekh
In krayzn do arim
Tsikopns fin dayn vig.
Dos pekl in der hant,
Dos hoyz in ash in brand;
Mir lozn zikh, mayn kind,
Zikhn glik.

Di velt hot got farmakht,
In imetim iz nakht—
Zi vart af indz
Mit shoyder in mit shrek.
Mir shteyen beyde do,
In shverer, shverer sho
In veysn nit vihin
S'firt der veg.

Men hot indz naket, bloyz
Faryogt fin indzer hoyz.
In fintsternish,
Getribn indz in feld,
In shturem, hogl, vint
Hot indz bagleyt, mayn kind,
Bagleyt indz inem opgrint
Fin der velt.

Close your little eyes,
Soon little birds will fly
In circles everywhere,
Around your cradle.
Your bundle in your hand,
Your house in ash and sand;
We leave you, my child,
In search for luck.

God closed the world,
Everywhere is night—

She waits for us
With horror and with dread.
We both are standing here,
At this difficult time,
Not knowing where
Our road is leading.

Stripped naked,
We were thrown from our home.
In the dark of night,
Driven out into the open field,
The wind and hail and storm
Accompanied us, my child,
Accompanied us into
The depths of the earth.

This lullaby was written by Isaiah Shpigl, a writer-poet-essayist-teacher who survived the Lodz ghetto and Auschwitz.[8] It was performed in the ghetto theater by the professional singer Ella Diament. The song has been published in several collections;[9] however only two survivors I interviewed, Lucille Eichengreen and Miriam Harel, were able to recall any part of it.

The lullaby is one of the most popular song genres of Yiddish folk and theater music. The performance of lullabies had been a tradition in the Yiddish theater from its inception under Goldfadn in the mid-nineteenth century. In a typical Jewish lullaby, the mother soothes the child to sleep with promises of pleasant times to come. The father is usually absent, off making money for the child's education; his return, however, is said to be imminent. Shpigl's composition turns this concept upside down: Father will never come home. The child lies down to sleep in an open field at the mercy of the elements, his parents' house having been burned to the ground.

Nature does not smile on this Jewish child; rather, the world is full of horror. God has brought night into the little boy's world. The third verse strengthens the horror: "In the dark of night, / Driven out into the open fields, / The wind and hail and storm / Accompanied us, my child, / Accompanied us into depths of the earth."

According to Lucille Eichengreen, Rumkowski was in attendance during one of the performances of this song. He felt that the song manifested a pessimistic point of view of his "kingdom" and instructed the poet, "Bay mir vest mer nisht zingen" (you will never sing for me again). The song was forbidden and Shpigl was threatened with deportation. After some negotiation, he was allowed to remain in the ghetto but was transferred to a different workshop.

The music is a rare form of musical hybrid, a tango-lullaby. Evidently, tango melodies were so popular during this period that even tender lyrics could be set to them without seeming in the least incongruous.

Song 32

Nit kayn rozhinkes, nit kayn mandlen
(No More Raisins, No More Almonds)
Text: Isaiah Shpigl
Music: David Beyglman

Nit kayn rozhinkes in nit kayn mandlen.
Der tate iz nit geforn handlen,
Lyulinke mayn zun,
Lyulinke mayn zun.

Er hot farlozt indz in avek,
Vi di velt hot nor an ek,
Lyulinke, mayn zun,
Lyulinke, mayn zun.

S'shrayen soves, s'voyen velf,
Got, derbarem zikh un helf,
Lyulinke mayn zun,
Lyulinke mayn zun.

Ergets shteyt er in er vakht,
Mandlen, rozhinkes a sakh,
Lyulinke mayn zun,
Lyulinke mayn zun.

Kimen r'vet af zikher shoyn,
Zen dikh, kind, mayn eyntsik kroyn,
Lyulinke mayn zun,
Lyulinke mayn zun.

No raisins and no almonds.
Your father has not gone out trading,
Lu, lu, lu, my son,
Lu, lu, lu, my son.

He has left us, gone away,
To the end of the world,
Lu, lu, lu, my son,
Lu, lu, lu, my son.

Owls are screeching, wolves are howling,
God have pity on us and help us,
Lu, lu, lu, my son,
Lu, lu, lu, my son.

Somewhere he is standing, watching,
Lots of almonds and raisins,
Lu, lu, lu, my son,
Lu, lu, lu, my son.

There's no doubt that he will come,
To watch you, son, my only crown,
Lu, lu, lu, my son,
Lu, lu, lu, my son.

None of the informants I interviewed recalls this particular song. However, it can be found in the published collections of Kaczerginsky (1948: 93, 387) and Mlotek and Gottlieb (1983: 62–63). Like the previous song, it is a lullaby. According to Kaczerginsky, it was written after the death of Shpigl's daughter, Eva.

The song is a "negative" version of Goldfadn's lullaby "Rozhinkes mit mandlen" (Raisins and almonds), perhaps the best-known song of the Yiddish theater, if not of all Yiddish songs. Goldfadn's tender lyric (based in turn on a whole corpus of "Rozhinkes" in Yiddish folklore) asks the sweet child to sleep well; his father has gone to market, and when he returns he will bring raisins and almonds. The little boy will grow up to be a scholar.[10]

The ghetto version, however, declares: No raisins, no almonds, father (who has not gone trading) will never come back home. Where did he go? To the world's end. Nature is personified; owls and wolves identify and sympathize with the man going "who knows where." The music does not quote or parody Goldfadn's original tune or any of the many "Rozhinkes" folk melodies.

Song 33

Tsigaynerlid (Gypsy Song)

Text and music: David Beyglman

Fintster di nakht,
Vi koyln shvarts,
Nor trakht in trakht,
In s'klapt mayn harts:
Mir tsigayner, leybn vi keyner,
Mir laydn noyt,
Genug koym oyf broyt.

Refren:
Dzum, dzum, dzum . . .
Mir flien arim vi di tchaykes.
Dzum, dzum, dzum . . .
Mir shpiln oyf di balalaykes.

Nit vi men tugt,
Nit vi men nakht.
Yeder zikh plogt,
Not trakht in trakht:
Mir tsigayner leybn vi keyener,
Mir laydn noyt,
Genug koym oyf broyt.

Refren:
Dzum, dzum, dzum . . .

Dark is the night,
Like black coal.
I think and think,
And my heart pounds:
We Gypsies live like nobody else,
We suffer pain,
From lack of bread.

Refrain:
Dzum, dzum, dzum . . .
We fly like seagulls.
Dzum, dzum, dzum . . .
We play the balalaikas.

Nowhere to stay,
Nowhere to be.
Everyone struggles,
But I just think:
We Gypsies live like nobody else,

We suffer pain,
From lack of bread.

Refrain:
Dzum, dzum, dzum . . .

As with the previous number, this song was first published in Kaczerginsky's collection (and also appears in a more recent publication by Kalisch); [11] again, none of my informants recalled this particular ghetto song.

The song concerns the fate of the inmates of the Gypsy camp in Lodz, who were brought to the ghetto in 1941 and were liquidated soon thereafter. It describes the gypsies' attempts to combat suffering with singing and dancing. The tragedy of these gypsies elicited the sympathy of the Jewish inmates.[12]

The song imitates the "Gypsy manner," a style made popular by Liszt and his followers in the nineteenth century. It is set in a minor key (with augmented seventh), with a slow verse followed by a brisk, dancelike refrain. It is within the genre of "exotic" or "ethnic" songs of the Yiddish theater using Rumanian, Russian, and other tunes to introduce a "foreign exotic flavor." [13]

The Youth Organization

The recollections of two survivors, Leah Hochberg and Arieh Tal-Shir, best represent the songs and attitudes of members of the ghetto's various youth organizations. Both Leah and Arieh were members of Gordonya, a youth group named in honor of the progressive Zionist Socialist Aharon David Gordon (1856–1922). Although I interviewed members of other youth organizations, most of my survivors belonged to the Gordonya movement, which was very active in Lodz during the twenties and thirties; I have thus concentrated on songs from this group.

Leah Hochberg first joined the Gordonya Organization in 1937, becoming a member of the *Hakhsharah* (youth training camp) in the Lodz ghetto in 1940. Arieh Tishler (later Tal-Shir) was Leah's Gordonya counselor in the ghetto.[14]

Leah's Story

Leah, née Luća Boronshtein, was born in Alexandrow, Poland, in 1925, shortly before her family moved to Lodz. She completed her elementary education in a Polish school and, prior to the onset of hostilities, she also studied Hebrew. When the ghetto was sealed,

Shlomo Flam and friends playing the harmonica in Marysin at a youth organization gathering, 1941. Shlomo Flam Collection.

she joined the Gordonya *Hakhsharah,* taking part in its activities until 1941. Following this she worked in the *Teppich Ressort,* the ghetto carpet factory, where she made carpets until 1944. From Lodz she was transported to Auschwitz, then to Bergen-Belsen, and finally to a labor camp where she was liberated by the American army. Of her entire family only Leah and one of her younger sisters survived the war.

Leah immigrated to Israel in 1948, where she lives in Kibbutz Maale HaḤamisha with her husband and family. She is in charge of the *kibbutz* archives, which focus on Holocaust material; she also organizes the annual Holocaust commemoration ceremonies of the *kibbutz.*

Most of the members of Gordonya, not unexpectedly, share common attitudes and memories. The idea of collectives (Heb.: *kvutsah*), the organization's central ideology, had its impact on the members, and the recollections of the Gordonya youth are essentially positive and optimistic. (This is true, I found, for most survivors who had belonged to the youth groups.)

Leah vividly remembered her days and nights in the *Hakhsharah:*

> During weekdays we sat together, and in the evenings we sang songs by the light of a small burner. Every meeting we learned a new song. The leader of all that was Arieh Tal-Shir (Tishler), of course. We sang

in Hebrew without knowing the language that well; we transliterated the words into Latin characters. Arieh taught us the songs and he sang, too. He used to sing a lot and we joined him in singing, and that's how we learned the songs. He also sang many songs in Yiddish, such as "By mayn fentster shteyt oyvn vayse toybn tsvay" [Above my window, two doves are standing],[15] but I do not recall the end of the song. This song is full of hope and romance, and this was what nourished us. Because of our singing we could spiritually escape the ghetto. We sang and listened to the songs and stories of *Eretz-Yisrael,* we learned about the events which had taken place there, we even had a contact person in the beginning who updated us with what was going on there. In the very beginning of the ghetto times, we even received postcards and some packages with sweets from Palestine. I remember once receiving a package which was impossible to divide evenly among us so we sold it and used the money for other things.

The strong ideology that emphasized the group over the individual, the sharing and working together for immediate survival and even more so for the future, formed the core idea and gave cohesion to the youth organizations. It suited the needs of these young people, and helped them retain their morale during those most trying times.

Leah recalled one special night:

It was a Hanukkah evening in 1941. We gathered in the dining room of the training area, which was full of people from our group as well as from other organizations. And we were sailing beyond reality, we crossed the Mediterranean, we reached the Jordan River! These are things which left a strong impression in my heart and in my memory. We sang Bialik songs, one member recited a poem written by Uri Zvi Greenberg, another member received a poem by Saul Tchernichowsky, and we lit the candles. We remembered the Maccabees. It was a very impressive evening for us as hosts, and for our guests. And there was another performance, Miriam [Harel] sang a song by Tchernichowsky, "Saḥki saḥki" [Play, play], and others sang and recited. . . . I remember it as if it were today.

Falling back on historical Jewish archetypes was a means of comfort during those cataclysmic times. The story of the Maccabees refers both to the destruction of the First Temple in Jerusalem and to Jewish heroism throughout the ages. The preservation of group memory at a time of radical transition was the core of the event reported by Leah. The collective memory passed through the rituals, prayers, and literary archetypes of the East European Jews and continued in the ghetto youths' celebration of Hanukkah.

Leah remembered cultural and social activities—lectures, reading, and singing. When she explained the proportion of time devoted to the different activities she remarked: "How much can one do of each activity? Time is limited. One cannot listen to lectures, or play games all the time. One cannot read all the time, and besides in the evening there was not enough light for reading. So we sat in the darkness and sang. We sang and sang."

All these youth activities took place before the end of 1941. Thereafter Rumkowski ordered the *Hakhsharah* closed and every member sent home. Leah recalled only a few meetings in private homes after the closing: two took place at Arieh's home, with only a few people participating. As Leah described it: "We did not give up singing. It was singing for its own sake. We sang all kinds of songs. Actually, we did not have any good news to talk about. We tried to forget the bad times, so we sang. It worked wonderfully! I think it was one of the things which helped us to survive."

Leah felt the need to amplify this last statement for me. She explained, "The problem of physical hunger is not so difficult as psychological hunger. It is common knowledge that a hungry person is not hungry in his stomach but in his head. There is no doubt that the singing helped."

Singing as a means of escape, as a cure for the psychological trauma of the ghetto, is the theme of Leah's testimony. She spoke in favor of Rumkowski and his positive attitude toward children and youth. She herself was confined for one week in the ghetto's sanitarium when she had typhus; her sister (on Leah's request) remained for two weeks. The sanitarium was supervised by Rumkowski's wife. Leah refused to make hasty conclusions concerning Rumkowski's actions. She believed that to head the Jewish community at this time was a very difficult task. She did not feel one would have taken that position purely out of a lust for power.

She also remembered the weaving she had done in the workshop, where she actually became a counselor after a while. Weaving became her first profession. She remarks that although she learned it in the ghetto, she still enjoys weaving and is proud of the art pieces which decorate her house. Weaving in the ghetto period was done with leftovers and odd pieces. "To my great sorrow, we wove cloth which came back to the ghetto after the transports were taken away, very often with bloodstains. It was terrible."

She did not recall singing in the workshop. She did remember the efforts she made under the influence of other laborers who belonged to the Communist Youth Movement to slow down the work. She believed that an individual could not accomplish much under those circumstances, that only a group could succeed. She, therefore, joined

Rumkowski visiting the youth organization's *Hakhsharah.* Shlomo Flam Collection.

the Communist Youth Organization. She feels guilty for doing that (after all, she was a Gordonya member), and to explain her action says, "To justify my collaboration with the Communist movement, I say that any person who was not a little 'red' when he was young is not a sensitive human being when he is old."

Leah felt the need to justify her association with a non-Gordonya group, since loyalty to the ideology of one's organization was, even within the constraints of the ghetto, a strongly affirmative act.

And Leah repeated the central theme of her life in the ghetto: "Spiritually, I was in another place. Consciously and unconsciously."

Arieh's Story

Arieh Tal-Shir was born in Lodz in 1918. He came from a Zionist family; however, he spoke Yiddish in his childhood, later studying Polish and Hebrew. In 1935 he went to Sosnowiec, Vilna, and Będzin to receive training as a counselor for the Gordonya Youth Organization. In this period he also met Jewish young people from many places in Poland, whom he tried to convince to join the organization. In 1939 he returned to Lodz and remained there until 1944. Toward the end of 1944 he was transported to a labor camp in Lesksenhausen, where he was liberated in 1945. His mother was taken in

1942, and his younger sister died in the ghetto. His father, brother, and older sister survived.

After liberation, Arieh returned to Poland and helped to organize survivors who wanted to immigrate to Israel. In 1947 he embarked from Italy on a ship that took him to Israel. Arieh now lives in Beersheba, is married, and has three children. In Israel he changed his last name, Tishler, to a Hebrew homologue, Tal-Shir.

Arieh, a counselor whom so many apprentices admired, is a very modest man. Though happy to share his personal story with me, he was convinced that his contribution to my study would be very limited.

He began his story in 1935, when he was traveling about Poland for Gordonya:

> Today when someone wants to be entertained, he buys a ticket and goes to the movies, or to the theater, or he can stay at home and turn on the television. Back then in the thirties the only equipment available for entertainment was a radio, and only a few people could own one. The lives of Jewish people were different, and difficult. All the Polish Jews suffered from the oppression of the government. Most of the Jews of Poland were poor, were beggars. Many Jews lived in small *shtetls* [Yidd.: small towns]. They had no hope, but if they had known this maybe they would have committed suicide. This explains why young people joined the *Hakhsharah* for four and five years. The young people who came to the *Hakhsharah* came to prepare themselves for collective life in Israel. They came from ordinary homes. But in training, they took the most despised jobs, cutting wood and carrying water. Spoiled girls worked as housekeepers and in factories, and all lived in the collective camp. In the big cities they organized communes, but in the small *shtetls* it was more difficult. Imagine at sixteen living with your parents and then suddenly going to live in a collective and having to cook for thirty people on a paraffin cooking stove.
>
> But we are talking about "Why did they sing?" So, in the evening, when the youth gathered, there was belief and a need for cultural life. People had to read. People organized celebrations for holidays, for Sabbath and for every other occasion—or for no occasion. And we were singing. We had in mind the stories about the people already living in Israel who did not have enough to eat, and yet were also singing. So we sang, and whoever had a nice, good voice became the center of the group. So please do not exaggerate.

Arieh thought that his apprentices exaggerated in describing his talent and main role as the singing master. He first believed that I was placing too much importance on songs and singing in the ghetto. But he continued to describe the singing, realizing while he spoke that it was indeed a major part of his life:

> Anyhow, singing together was a very common and favorite activity. It was a means to create social consolidation. We used to sit in the evenings, after talking about different issues, different subjects, and we sang. We sang a lot. We also studied Hebrew, and this was the core of our social life. In the youth organizations we had our "aristocratic" members. They were the members who studied Hebrew, and were seen as being closer to Israel. . . . We were all "like angels," in that we believed that we are going to a new world, going to have a better future. And we organized and wove this dream over all those years.

The youth organization's *Hakhsharah,* in its prewar form, continued for nine months in the ghetto. Arieh wanted to conclude the interview: "This is my short answer about the singing question. Did I talk much about singing?" I did not let him stop, however, but asked about the content of the songs. He explained:

> Listen, we were living our lives, we drew all our strength from the fact that we were not living in the present. Very often our apprentices complained that they felt very guilty when they visited their homes [every week], and saw their parents suffer—they themselves had it relatively good. We were working and had some agriculture in addition to our food rations. In a normal family, when someone is sick, he takes from those who are healthy. But we were a "family" of young and healthy people. We had a very intensive agenda: in the morning we cleaned our rooms, attended lectures, worked, assembled again, and started singing. We sang all the songs which are known now in Israel as "Shirey Tnu'ot Ha'no'ar" [Songs of the youth organizations].[16]

Arieh paused and recited some of those songs: "We also exchanged songs. Youth coming from places closer to Russia brought their Ukrainian songs. Others brought Hassidic tunes, others brought Polish songs. Some also brought dilettante arrangements of songs. That's it."

Arieh did not recall street songs, or theater songs. As he observed, "I did not live in this world." He worked in a carpentry factory, but he did not live in the world of the workshop either:

> I became a supervisor in our carpentry factory. I studied to be a carpenter before the war. The hunger in the ghetto was great, one would have paid a lot for a bowl of soup. So it is natural that smuggling wood flourished. People became very sophisticated doing that. . . . The workers got a sack of wood shavings and the weight had to be checked. Many times they smuggled some pieces of wood for heating the cold houses. I supervised their work very strictly but not their smuggling.

> One day my boss invited me for a talk and said to me: "Why are you so good to your workers? Do you think that when the ghetto is opened again, and you reach *Eretz-Yisrael*, that you will be able to write it down to your merit?" Even he knew that I was not really there in the workshop, but somewhere else: in Israel. Unconsciously, it made life easier.

Although both Leah and Arieh share the same ideology, and took part in the same activities of the same youth organization, their attitudes are somehow different, perhaps as a result of their ages: Leah was a teenager during those times, while Arieh was already a young man. Leah therefore seems more optimistic speaking about her ghetto experiences, while Arieh is more cynical, trying to view the past as an experienced man who knew much about life before entering the ghetto. The ghetto was an episode in his life. Perhaps the slight difference in views represents the general difference of their characters.

For both of them, however, the youth organization's activities in general and singing in particular served as a vehicle to escape from the hardships of the life of the ghetto to the dream of a better future life.

The Songs of Gordonya

Group singing inevitably opened and closed each meeting of the youth organizations. Participants sang mainly in Hebrew, but also in the variety of languages brought from their various homelands. This repertoire comprised prewar songs in Yiddish, Russian, Polish, Czech, and Ukrainian.

Possibly because members drew from the established Hebrew song repertoire, original songs were not created in the youth organizations. I will therefore only touch briefly on this repertoire, in order to suggest the variety of songs performed in the context of youth organizations.

Of the many youth organization songs Arieh recalls, the following were particularly popular during the ghetto period: "O'lim" (Immigrants), composed by Shneor Postolski, was written in the early 1930s, and describes the return of the pioneers to Palestine; "Anu nihiyeh harishonim" (We shall be the first) was another pioneers' song; "Shama'ti maa'siyah" (I heard a story), a folksong which originated in Yavneel, Palestine, tells about two lovers in the barn; "Ruaḥ a'tsuv" (Sad wind) was a love song by Yitzḥak Katzenelson; "Yad a'nugah" (Tender hand) was a love poem Zalman Shneor adapted to a Palestinian-Arab melody; and "Shir haḥotsvim" (The song of the quarrymen) was a love song Arieh learned in 1933.

A humorous song (previously unknown to me), of which Arieh recalls four lines in Hebrew, can serve as a typical example of the genre of Hebrew youth organization's songs:

Be'eretz yisrael mukhraḥim lisbol,
Ani ohevet vesovelet,
Ve'atah einkha margish.
Praḥim li liktof etse
Ki bapraḥim et libi arape

In *Eretz-Yisrael* one has to suffer,
I love and suffer,
And you don't care.
Flowers I will pick up
And with flowers I will heal my wounded heart.

In addition, Arieh recalls singing songs, including love songs, to lyrics by the famous poet Chaim Nachman Bialik. He also remembers singing the patriotic hymn "Birkat a'm" (Bless the people), also known as "Teḥezaknah"; the Jewish national anthem "Hatikvah" (Our hope); and some Hebrew lyrics sung to Russian melodies.

Arieh Tal-Shir, his younger brother, Yeḥiel, and their apprentices Miriam Harel, Shlomo Flam, and Leah Hochberg also recalled certain Yiddish folksongs that were popular with the youth organizations. They named such melodies as "Margaritkelekh" (Daisies), "Hey, tsigelekh" (Hey, little goats), and others.[17]

The Tal-Shir brothers and Miriam Harel were known for their good voices. Many of my informants attested to the musical talent of these singers, though in general the individual excellence of singers was not mentioned.

Yeḥiel Tal-Shir (Tishler) was another counselor in the Gordonya Youth Organization who kept a songbook; this helped him to teach the songs he had collected to his students. He described the role of music in the Gordonya meetings thus: "Singing united the people. The members from Lodz and outside Lodz could communicate and feel as one group through singing."[18]

The songs he recalls are Yiddish and Russian folksongs and, interestingly, a fragment of a German marching song (dating probably from World War I):

Es geht alles vorüber
Es geht alles vorbei
Nach jedem Dezember
Kommt wieder der Mai.

Everything passes by
Everything passes away
Following every December
Comes again May.

This is a clear-cut example of an optimistic song, offering the hope that all troubles will soon dissipate and that better times will arrive soon. (I asked Yeḥiel if it bothered him to sing a German song during the occupation. He ironically replied: "No, it was just another song.")

Miriam Harel also recalled in detail a Yiddish song titled "Zol zayn" (What if), written by Papiernikov to a traditional Yiddish folk melody.[19] As Miriam describes it, "the song encompassed the philosophy of the Jewish people. It says, I have to reach the opposite shore, I have to keep going and not give up, because the light of hope is living inside me and tells me to go."

The content of the youth organization songs was never topical (as with the street songs), nor truly political, except to the extent that singing in Hebrew was a political statement of sorts. Instead it reflected the participants' hopes and dreams for a better future in a free land, in *Eretz-Yisrael.* Indeed, after the war many members of the Zionist youth organizations immigrated to Israel.

The Workplace

All the subjects I interviewed worked in a workshop or a factory established by Rumkowski in order to survive. Few were able to cope with the hardships of the ghetto without the rations of bread and soup the workshops (referred to as *Ressorts* by the survivors) provided. Work meant food and therefore survival in the ghetto.

For those born in Lodz, a city known for its blue-collar workers and industries, work was a way of life even before the war. All ghetto dwellers had to work or they were subject to resettlement, which came to be synonymous with death.

No informant recalls singing as an important event in this context, and none could recall performances staged in the workplace. Laboring in unsuitable conditions under pressure and hunger apparently left no time for singing.

Thus, accounts of singing are few and brief, and the songs I collected are fragmented. Most of the informants say, "Yes there was some singing but I cannot recall the songs," or, "No, there was no singing; who could sing while working so hard?" Yet, two of the survivors did recollect some fragments of songs from the workplace:

Song 34

Song of the Children's Workplace

Freda Rapoport (née Burns, b. 1929) worked sewing brassieres and later uniforms in the children's workplace. As she recalled, more than a thousand children worked there under the supervision of a Mr. Glazer. She remembered a song in Yiddish, composed in the workplace, that described the quality of the products the workers produced. However she could not remember the melody, except for some fragments:

Mir zenen *uczennice*
Fun glazer's resort,
In geto farnemtmen
Dos ershter ort.
Hay di li ya da . . .
Mir danken dir her prezes,
Di fin di ort geshafn
Host undz *pazet*
Dos yugentlikher resort.

We are students
Of Glazer's workshop,
In the ghetto we take
The first pride of place.
Hay di li ya da . . .
We thank you, Mr. President,
Who established this place
And trained us,
The youth resort.

According to Freda, the conditions in 1942 were very reasonable, and the workers were allowed extra food rations. Later, conditions grew worse. In this song they are grateful to Rumkowski ("Mr. President") and proud of being workers at this specific workplace.

Freda (thirteen years old when she began working at the *Ressort*) recalled a similar song in Polish in which the workers complain about their boss, Glazer, saying that although he was a good director, he stole the children's extra food rations. She could not, however, recall specific lyrics or music. (In the present song fragments, *uczennice* and *pazet* are Polish words.)

Interestingly, Freda remarks that in general the content of a song was secondary; its prime importance was that it was something to sing: "We sang all day long."

Song 35
Song of the Millinery Workplace

For four years (1940–44), Itka Slodowsky worked in the millinery workshop, a factory for the manufacture of hats. She recalls a song in Polish composed by one of her coworkers in 1943, describing "special orders" received by the factory:

Solo: Raz przyszła pani Arbuz
Chór: Popatrz, popatrz, popatrz!
Solo: Zrobiła czapke "Tadelos"
Chór: Popatrz, popatrz, popatrz!
Solo: Do miasta ją wysłała
Chór: Popatrz, popatrz, popatrz!
Solo: Czapka się spodobała
Chór: Co jak tak o, o, o,
Jak dobrze pani Arbuz, o, o, o,
Jak dobrze!

Solo: I przyszło zamówienie
Chór: Popatrz, popatrz, popatrz!
Solo: Srzerząc zadowolenie
Chór: Popatrz, popatrz, popatrz!
Solo: Więc Arbuz wszystkich budzi
Chór: Popatrz, popatrz, popatrz!
Solo: Dajcież mi zdolnych ludzi
Chór: Co jak tak o, o, o,
Jak dobrze pani Arbuz, o, o, o,
Jak dobrze!

Solo: Once came Mrs. Arbuz—
Chorus: Look, look, look!
Solo: She made a hat so easily—
Chorus: Look, look, look!
Solo: She sent it to the city—
Chorus: Look, look, look!
Solo: The hat pleased everybody
Chorus: Like this, oh, oh, oh!
Very good, Mrs. Arbuz,
Very good!

Solo: An order came in—
Chorus: Look, look, look!
Solo: They are so very pleased—
Chorus: Look, look, look!
Solo: Mrs. Arbuz wakes up everybody—
Chorus: Look, look, look!

Solo: Give me good workers
Chorus: Like this, oh, oh, oh!
Very good, Mrs. Arbuz,
Very good!

The song tells about Mrs. Arbuz, director of the hat factory. She created a model for a children's hat, and sent it to the Germans who declared themselves very pleased with it. As a result, the workshop received an order for children's hats, which in turn pleased the workers, who held to the belief that the more they worked the longer they would live. Following the acceptance of the order, Mrs. Arbuz pompously demanded more "professional" workers for her workshop so that she would be able to fill the order.

This is another example of a song which relates to a specific situation and place within the ghetto. The melody, in a minor key and duple meter, is reminiscent of the folk style, and is likely a contrafact on a Polish folksong.

Song 36

Song of the Low Stream Workplace

Itka Slodowsky has been collecting ghetto songs for her own personal use for the last ten years. In the course of her collecting she encountered a song from the *Shvakh shtrum* (Yidd.: "Low stream") workplace, which manufactured telephone headpieces.

Getunya, getunya klap

Getunya, getunya klap!
Men arbet bay tug in bay nakht,
Her prezes, es kumt aykh a dank
Blayb mit indz oy leybn lang!
Oy geto oy geto klap!

Der kenig fun resortn
Iz oykh tsi indz gekimen,
In hot di gantse arbet
In zayne hent genimen.

Kuk tsi, her Yakobovitz,
Vi arbeytn indzere hent,
Azoy geyt adurkh a tug nokh a tug
Tsvishn di groye vent.

Getunya, getunya clap!
We labor day and night,
Mr. President, we owe you thanks

Stay with us and long life to you
Oy ghetto oy ghetto clap!

The king of the *Ressorts*
Came to us to visit,
And took all of our work
Into his own hands.

Look, Mr. Jakubowicz,
How our hands are working,
That is how we pass the days
Between the grey walls.

According to Itka, who has no source for the song, the song continues in Polish (Itka has only fragments of the Polish text). The song is set to a famous Yiddish song "Tsum hemerl" (To the hammer), with text by Avraham Reisen and music by A. Bernstein. It was a workers' song composed in the first years of the twentieth century. It describes the plight of a poor cobbler who sings to his hammer in order to work faster. The cobbler's family is hungry; if his hammer refuses to work, they will starve.[20]

The ghetto version refers to the original song by using the call *klap* (hit), to keep up the rhythmic pace of production. The interns were well aware that should the workplace close down, everyone would be resettled, i.e., condemned to death.

The song refers to Rumkowski's express desire that "the ghetto run like clockwork." It also mentions the head of the Central Workshop Bureau, Aron Jakubowicz, whose power and visibility grew with the productivity of the ghetto in such a way that, toward the end of the ghetto period, he was as powerful as Rumkowski, if not more so. The ghetto was indeed productive, with many factories producing articles for German consumption. For the worker/singer of this topical song, just as for the cobbler of the song's original, work meant survival.

Summary

In these "other contexts" for singing, various genres of songs came into being to serve a variety of functions. Theater songs were performed on stage in front of an audience. Most of the songs had formed a part of the Yiddish theater repertoire before the war and were found suitable within the ghetto context, or made suitable by contrafact or parody technique. There were also original compositions introduced on the ghetto stage.

The themes of the songs are hunger, food (or lack of food), love, and the tragedy of the Jewish people. All the songs reflect the ghetto situation and changing moods of the people, from complete despair to expectant hope, often with a mixture of humor.

The youth organization songs largely excluded reflections of the present. These songs were on a different plane, close to the world of fantasy; they continued to reflect the original beliefs of the organization, despite the current events. Thus, in a socialist Zionist organization like Gordonya, the songs of the Hebrew repertoire concerned *Eretz-Yisrael* in one aspect or another. A second genre included nostalgic songs, which served to resuscitate sweet moments of the past.

At the workplace, the songs reflected everyday activities and events, but at the same time commented on the authorities and their policies. These songs dealt with the microcosm of the workshops, and touched only in general on outside happenings. They were sung in the languages best known to their audience, mainly Polish but often Yiddish.

Thus the three contexts for singing generated three different types of expression: a personal-artistic one elicited by the overall situation; a group-ideological expression negating the present situation in order to depict a shining future; and a group expression of local specific occurrences.

Several songs were actually composed (text and music) in the Lodz ghetto. Three that I discuss in this context (songs 31, 32, 33) are two lullabies which were popularized by professional singers after the war, and a Yiddish dance song dedicated to the Gypsies of the Lodz ghetto. Other songs were composed in the theater style, though my sources could not testify whether they were performed in the ghetto.[21] The rest of the ghetto's theater repertoire derived from the stock of prewar Yiddish songs.

As with other European and American Yiddish popular music, the songs' composers preferred the minor mode. In the ghetto theater songs, however, unlike the "outside" Yiddish theater repertoire (especially in America), no particular "symbolic" use was made of the augmented second scale.

The songs had a central role in the show, although since the show's success did not depend on ticket sale (as most of the tickets were distributed among the workers of the workshops), the availability of the material and performers defined the performance.

The youth organizations drew their songs from various sources: Israeli music (with its Arabic inflections), Russian workers' songs, and Yiddish folk tunes. None of these tunes was created in the ghetto.

The few workplace songs that have come down to us are either parodies of Polish folk or popular melodies or (in the case of song 36) a contrafact of a Yiddish popular labor song. With such a small body of surviving works, however, it is difficult to draw persuasive conclusions from the study of the workplace repertoire.

NOTES

1. Interview with Pinchas Shaar, New York, 19 October 1986.

2. Henryk Neftalin was one of the founders of the ghetto's archives and defined its goals; he wanted to create a basis of source materials for future scholars (Dobroszycki 1984: x).

3. Mordechai Gebirtig was shot by the Germans on 4 June 1942. This song may be found in Gebirtig's collection of songs, *Mayne Lider* (1948: 66–67).

4. The song was remembered by Yaakov Flam, Shlomo Flam, Avraham Weberman, Arieh Shaar, and others.

5. Interview with Yosef Mulaz, Kiryat Bialik, 28 March 1985.

6. Polish words are given in Yiddish transcription or pronunciation.

7. Other popular versions of this dialogue song sing of girls with names like Rifkele, Brayndele, Neḥamele, Khaye-Sorele, Shifkele, Rokhele; see Beregovski 1982: no. 19; Cahan 1957: nos. 93–94; Dobrushin-Yuditski 1940: no. 59; Ginsburg-Marek 1901: no. 138; Idelsohn 1932b: nos. 285, 522; Kaufmann 1986: no. 28; Kipnis 1949: 21; Rubin 1979: 89. A recent album, *Folksong in the East European Jewish Tradition from Mariam Nirenberg* (1986), song 19, provides another version. Some versions repeat the second half of the male dialogue.

8. Until his death in July 1990, Isaiah Shpigl had been living in Israel, where he resumed his writing career in Yiddish. He published his novels and poems written before his internment in the ghetto, as well as those written after his liberation; see Bibliography.

9. The song "Makh tsi die eygelekh" can be found in: Kaczerginsky 1948: 92; Mlotek and Gottlieb 1983: 52. The transcription and translations I give here are based on Mlotek and Gottlieb's version.

10. On lullabies in the Yiddish folksong tradition see Y. L. Cahan (1952, 1957) and Ruth Rubin (1965, 1979); see also Gefen (1986), a recent book in Hebrew dedicated to the songtexts of Yiddish lullabies.

11. "Tsigaynerlid" was published by Kaczerginsky (1948: 41, 370), and in Shoshana Kalisch's collection (1985: 87–91), taken from Kaczerginsky.

12. On the tragic fate of the Gypsies, the *Chronicle* dedicates several entries: November 1941 (Dobroszycki 1984: 82); December 1941 (1984: 85); January 1942 (1984: 107). Yaakov Rotenberg describes their destiny (see above, Chapter 3), as do Yaakov Flam, Abraham Weberman, and others.

13. On this genre see Slobin (1982: 35–40).

14. Interviews were conducted in Hebrew in the interviewees' homes. Arieh Tal-Shir was interviewed in August 1985 and Leah Hochberg in August 1986.

15. Leah probably refers to a Yiddish love song, titled in Ruth Rubin's anthology (1965 : 70–71) as "Tsvey taybelekh" (Two little doves). The song tells about two lovers who are parted.

16. These songs were published on Israeli records entitled *Shirat hano'ar* (Songs of the youth), Israel MFI 31076; and *Nostalgia*, Hataklit 20015–16, 1975.

17. These Yiddish folksongs can be found in Mlotek's anthology of Yiddish folksongs (1972). "Margaritkelekh" was a popular song written by the famous Hebrew Yiddish poet Zalman Shneor in 1909 (Mlotek 1977 : 40–41); "Hey, tsigelekh" is attributed to Mordechai Gebirtig (Mlotek 1977 : 213). These songs were published in earlier collections as well.

18. Interview with Yeḥiel Tal Shir, Jerusalem, 20 August 1985.

19. "Zol zayn" is published in Mlotek's collection (1972 : 186–87); according to Mlotek it was written in the early 1920s. Joseph Papiernikov was born in Warsaw in 1899 and settled in Palestine in 1924. He was one of the pioneers of Yiddish poetry in Israel.

20. "Tsum hemerl" is published in Mlotek's collection (1972 : 78–79). Mlotek notes that the song became very popular in Europe and the United States.

21. I have found another song, published in both *30 Ghetto-Lieder*, a collection of sheet music edited by Henek Kahn (New York, 1960 : song 15), and in Kaczerginsky's anthology *Songs of the Ghettos and Concentration Camps* (1948 : 60 and 374). The song is titled "Zamdn glien oyf der zun" (Sand glows in the sun) and was composed by A. Volman and D. Beyglman; according to Kaczerginsky it was composed in Lodz ghetto. The song does not directly refer to ghetto times, nor was it remembered by any of my informants, therefore I did not include it here. Kaczerginsky includes five additional songs from the Lodz ghetto which were not mentioned by the informants whom I interviewed. They were probably sung in the revue theater. Most of them have no reference to ghetto events. "A yiddish lidl" (A Yiddish song) (Kaczerginsky 1948 : 42–43) had text and music composed by David Beyglman. Only the text is published and I included it in the epilogue of this book. "Klayner volkn" (Small clouds) (Kaczerginsky 1948 : 66–67 and 377) had text written by the poet Y. Yachimovitz and music composed by David Beyglman. "Kinder yorn" (Childhood days) (Kaczerginsky 1948 : 68 and 378) featured text and music by David Beyglman. "Shpiglt zikh oyf shoiv di zun" (The sun reflects in a pane) (Kaczerginsky 1948 : 86) had text by Y. Yachimovitz and music by David Beyglman. Finally, "Dos shnayderl" (The tailor) was composed by Shimeon Yanovski, who wrote review pieces, and music composed by David Beyglman (Kaczerginsky 1948 : 171 and 400).

6

The Contemporary Context: Commemoration Ceremonies

Yizkor

So far in this book I have described the different functions of song in the ghetto. People sang for entertainment, to allow themselves political and topical references they were otherwise denied. Singing helped to focus the individual's despair, anger, and hope; it expressed the dream, the fantasy of escape; it served to submerge the individual into the group and thus dilute his or her suffering. But over and above these different considerations was one common denominator: the ghetto inhabitants sang for survival. Their song was the human voice crying out for recognition in an inhuman environment.

Many songs were sung within the walls of the ghetto. Some were composed there, while others, part of a prewar repertoire, were found suitable, or made to suit the life in the ghetto. The inhabitants sang in their homes, for the family, or in public; ghetto youth gathered together for group singing during their youth organization meetings, actors and singers sang on stage, and workers would accompany their routine with song.

Today, the stories and songs of the ghetto endure as a mandate to the world at large—and the Jewish world in particular—to remember and to commemorate. To remember these songs is to recall the ghetto dwellers' struggle for survival. Therefore, we must add a new function of song to those already discussed: commemoration. This final context of the Holocaust song takes us from the streets and institutions of the ghetto to the present day.

The focus of the Holocaust song today is not on the individual, but on manifestations of collective memory, on commemoration services, on the community (or the "communitas").[1] The questions addressed in this chapter concern the ultimate fate of the ghetto repertoire. What made certain songs suitable for reuse as ritual? What is the symbolic content of the songs? What values are inherent in the songs that qualify them for the new function as commemorative music? How does the surviving Lodz community redefine itself in the new context, and how does it manifest itself in song?

I will answer these questions through observation of the Lodz survivors' commemoration ceremonies. But, first I would like to introduce the notion of collective memory and its application in Jewish thought and culture. This concept is essential to the understanding of the contemporary commemorative context.

David Roskies, in his important book *Against the Apocalypse,* explains what is at the core of the Jewish collective memory of the Holocaust: "When the unit of destruction is not the individual but the collective, when the entire Jewish population of a town or a city is gone, and when the disappearance of each community is known by date, and there are dates enough to fill the calendar, then the task of remembrance threatens to eclipse all else. Yet the remnants of that same collective, those who feel the loss most keenly, manage to incorporate even so vast a destruction" (1984:4).

The collective memory of catastrophe has affected Jewish consciousness since the destruction of the First Temple. It has shaped Jewish literature, folklore, and customs from biblical times to the present. Roskies suggests that the Holocaust may have been the major breaking point in the history of Jewish culture, but that break had been anticipated over time by Jewish writers and poets whose legacy was an art culture capable of dealing with such mass destruction, however painfully. Thus, despite the decimation of the culture, its well-established means of handling catastrophe through art functioned and survived intact.

The Holocaust brought to an end the culture of the East European Jews. Most of the survivors immigrated to Israel and North America, bearing forever their past, their "ruined cities of the mind" (Roskies 1984:1). The keys to the gates of these metaphorical cities were preserved and passed on to the next generation through oral and written tradition, through stories, songs, pictures, and paintings. God's commandment *veshinantam levanekha* (Deut. 6:7), "tell your children," has been the obligation of the Jewish father since the exodus from Egypt. And, thus, the story of the recent destruction had to be told. First, however, the teachers themselves needed to understand.

The survivors did perceive that group memory was now something precious. The survivors, wherever they finally resettled, searched for their *landsmen* (people from the same hometown); many set up *landsmanshaftn* (hometown associations) in their new countries.

These associations organized the collective response and maintained the collective memory as a living force. Each new organization issued a memorial book (*yizkor-bukh*) dedicated to the lost communities; each set aside a special day for remembrance and established a ritual for commemoration. In addition to these *landsmanshaftn* commemorations, there is a single collective commemoration day for all the victims of the Holocaust, observed as a national holiday in Israel.[2]

As the survivors' generation dwindles, their stories simplify. The Holocaust song, originally a coping mechanism, was transformed—both diminished and enlarged in the greater historical process which mythologized the Holocaust into a struggle between good and evil.

The Jews who mourn publicly, who preserve for the future a version of the Holocaust that is necessarily simplified, cannot allow the so-called trivia from the past to intrude on their solemnities. Thus the major part of the ghetto street songs, domestic music, and topical material dealing with individuals with names (such as "Rumkowski") must perish from the idealized version put forth in the ritual.

Removed from its historical context, the Holocaust achieved the status of a myth. Thus, the survivors commemorate "saints" and ignore the complexity of human nature. This is exemplified in the special collective *yizkor*, a prayer for the dead, composed in memory of the Jewish martyrs and recited on Holocaust commemoration days:

Yizkor elohim nishmot
Hakdoshim vehatehorim
Shenehergu, shenishḥetu veshenisrefu,
Veshenitbeu veshenehneku
Al kidush hashem. . . .
Al yedey hanazim ve'ozrehem—
Yimaḥ Shmam.

May God remember the souls
Of the saintly martyrs
Who have been slaughtered,
Burned, drowned or strangled
For their loyalty to God. . . .
By the Nazis and their collaborators—
May their name be blotted out, forever.[3]

For the purpose of this study, I observed several types of commemoration ceremonies; however, I will discuss only one in detail. Since the focus of my work was on the Lodz community, I thought it appropriate to investigate that community's commemoration ritual. Although I will discuss the complete event, the focus of my present remarks will be the repertoire of songs.

The Israeli Lodz *landsmanshaft* gathers twice a year. The first assembly takes place directly after New Year's, in the ten days between Rosh Hashanah and Yom Kippur, coincident with the liquidation of the Lodz ghetto in 1944.[4] These ten days between the high holidays are known in Jewish tradition as *A'seret Yemey Tshuvah,* days for remembering deceased family members. During this assembly (described in some detail below) the *landsmen* conduct a secular commemoration ceremony incorporating a variety of programs, and a short *yizkor* ceremony. The second gathering takes place on "Holocaust Day," the official day set aside as a secular national holiday. A liturgical *yizkor* ceremony is conducted at the Ḥulon cemetery where the *landsmen* assemble at a monument to the memory of their murdered brethren, which serves in place of individual gravesites. Thus, the observance melds the Jewish traditional way of commemoration with newly established secular practices of Israel.

The event I attended was held in a large local auditorium in Tel Aviv, on 20 September 1986 at 8:00 P.M. It was publicized in several Israeli newspapers and in letters sent to the two thousand Lodz *landsmanshaft* members. About a thousand people paid the entrance fee to attend the ceremony. The main theme of the year's ceremony was "the story of the individual survivor."

The participants arrived about half an hour before the scheduled event. All were survivors with their families. Many of them greeted one another, all conducting their conversations in Hebrew.

On stage were ten chairs, a table, flowers, and the Israeli flag. The stage was lit and the participants sat in the darkened auditorium. The president of the *landsmanshaft* greeted the participants and informed them about the coming program. He stressed that the audience should not applaud after any speeches or performances. Finally the cantor was invited to begin the formal *yizkor* ceremony.

The cantor recited the *El male raḥamim* and *Kaddish* (prayers recited also for the anniversary of a death) as the audience stood and responded "Amen."[5] Soft crying could be heard coming from several places in the auditorium.

The heart of the ceremony was a panel discussion on life in Lodz, moderated by a professional journalist. Nine participants, survivors of Lodz ghetto, including a Holocaust scholar, an educator, and a philosopher, were invited on stage. A short musical interval—a recorded modern Hassidic tune—preceded the discussion. The moderator asked the participants to tell their stories. He asked them not to be analytical, but rather to portray the Jewish life of Lodz through their own personal stories.

The first participant told of her Zionist-Hebraist education; another spoke of her education at the Broude Gymnasium in Lodz, from which she graduated in 1935. The moderator asked her whether the gymnasium was open to everyone, or just to the community's elite. The interviewee replied that she felt it was open to everyone; moreover, the rich students paid for the poor ones. Her statement caused disagreement among the audience and some of them made loud remarks. She tried to continue but was interrupted again and again. The discussion proved the durability of resentment stemming from class differences, a resentment which had not dissipated over the years. The moderator said: "Some of you are still bitter now that you could not study in this gymnasium, but we can't fix that now." There are no solutions to the many questions of the past. One thing, though, is certain: the more controversial an issue is, the more it lives in memory.

Other participants spoke of the youth organizations and the Hassidic life in Lodz. The former youth organization activist told of his group's fight against anti-Semitism. The Hassidic panel member told of the liberal secular environment in Lodz where he sought spiritual sustenance from his Hassidic *Rebbe.* When he told about the death of his *Rebbe,* he touched on a subject the others had tried to avoid: the Holocaust.

Following the panel discussion, Ḥava Albershtein, a well-known Israeli popular singer, presented the first part of the musical program. She opened with the song "Oyfn veg shteyt a boym" (On the path stands a tree).[6] Itsik Manger's text is based on Yiddish folk motives, and concerns a mother's love for her children. Manger was a popular Jewish Rumanian folk poet who spent most of his life in America. This song was very popular throughout the Yiddish-speaking world, and was also well known in Lodz. Its popularity comes from the fact that it deals with universal human experience: the child who grows up and must leave the nest. The singer chose to include it as a nostalgic song, not of a lost childhood but of a lost culture.

Albershtein's second selection was "Zol zayn" (What if) by Joseph Papiernikov, written in the early 1920s. This song, expressing optimistic hope, was sung in the ghetto mainly by Zionist youth organization members who recall it vividly (see above, Youth Organization Songs). In her anthology, Mlotek has paraphrased the content of the song: "Maybe I am building castles in the air; maybe my God does not really exist. But in my dream things are brighter, and the sky is bluer than blue. Maybe I won't attain my goal, maybe my ship won't reach the shore. I really don't care about getting there, I just want to travel along a sunny road."[7]

The third song was a recent Israeli composition titled "Neḥamah" (Heb.: Comfort), by Rachel Shapira and Nurit Hirsh. A song of consolation, the singer felt its soft, slow, soothing melodiousness somehow appropriate to the event.

The discussion continued with remarks made by a survivor who came from a prominent business family. He described the peddlers in the streets, the children who offered their merchandise to passersby, and the street singers and performers. He enjoined the audience to reminisce with him about their old hometown, speaking of people, streets, commodities, food, and articles of commerce in the familiar Lodzer jargon. This endless flow of associations brought laughter from the audience as they joined in his recollections.

The stories so far concerned life in Lodz before the ghetto. The next two panelists spoke about the ghetto proper. One's story dealt with the portraits of the ghetto's most famous photographer, Mendl Grossman. The lecturer, enlivening his talk with slides of Grossman's work, told a different "survival" story, "how these unique and precious photographic documents were preserved through the Holocaust and rescued after the war." The other speaker told a story of Chaim Widawski, the man who kept a radio hidden in his quarters, risking his life to keep in contact with the world outside.[8]

Lodz, forty-two years after its liquidation, was the theme of the following two stories. A scholar from Yad VaShem, the Holocaust research institute of Israel, told about the institute's program of collecting material. He gave a summary of the state of research on the Lodz ghetto, stating the need for more study of Lodz resistance activities. Survivors of the Lodz ghetto have often been accused of not having organized a front to resist the Nazis. The speaker confronted his audience with the question of why a Mordecai Anielewicz (the leader of the uprising of the Warsaw ghetto) or Abba Kovner (the leader of the partisans of Vilna) did not arise in Lodz. He offered only partial answers, calling for a *ḥeshbon nefesh* (Hebrew), a collective self-examination.

The last talk was given by a daughter of survivors. She emphasized the sadness of the several *yortsayts* for deceased family members throughout the year—not only on Holocaust Day.

No comments or summaries were made at the panel's conclusion.

The singer Hava Albershtein was invited on stage. She sang four songs, two in Hebrew and two in Yiddish. The first song was "Mikhtav meema" (A letter from Mother), a Hebrew revision of "A brivele der mamen" (A letter to Mother), a Yiddish song by S. Shmulewitz.[9] This "revision" of the song depicts a mother's concern for her son who has gone to war.

The second song was the humorous popular Yiddish number "Rabeynu tam" (Rabbi Tam),[10] by Itsik Manger and Hertz Rubin. Albershtein has performed this work for years and considers it to be a nostalgia piece.

The third song was the most famous lullaby of the Yiddish theater, Goldfadn's "Rozhinkes mit mandlen" (Raisins and almonds). The singer did not perform songs from the ghetto, such as the lullaby "Nit kayn rozhinkes, nit kayn mandlen" (No more raisins, no more almonds), the quasi-parody of the Goldfadn piece that might have been considered appropriate (see above, song 32).

Albershtein's last song was the contemporary Israeli ballad "Mi ha'ish" (Who is the man), a song of belief and hope, with a text taken from the Bible and music in the modern Hassidic style.

The moderator expressed his wish that future commemoration rituals should follow the form of the service just examined. Following this comment (to which there was general assent), the audience stood to sing the national anthem, "Hatikvah" (Our hope), which concludes every Israeli ceremony.

As the moderator's closing remarks indicated, this service differed from those of previous years. Unlike central ceremonies for the community at large which I have observed in Israel and in Los Angeles, no guest speakers or officials were invited to speak. No party politics were involved, nor were present community issues discussed. Though the auditorium was full, it held the aura of an intimate family gathering—survivors of Lodz who came to strengthen their collective memory and gain support while memorializing.

Unlike the central commemoration ceremony, which includes various messages to the broader Jewish community, not just Holocaust survivors, the *landsmanshaft* commemoration does not pretend to speak to outsiders. The participants came to remember and commemorate their unique Lodzer history. They came to conduct a dialogue with their past from their present experience as Jews who lived to witness the creation of an independent homeland.

As to the function of songs within the service, I have noted that none of the songs performed was composed in the ghetto or dealt specifically with ghetto times. This indeed reflects the "communitas" attitude toward its past, as opposed to the community's attitude toward the present. It now views itself first and foremost as Israeli, and as such refuses to dwell on the past, occupying itself instead with the ongoing process of reinforcing Jewish nationhood.

The survivors do not care to see their repertoire survive, and did not pass it on to their children. Thus, the two songs sung by Ḥava Albershterin served as generalized examples of Jewish hope and nostalgia.

What, then, is a Holocaust song today? For the *Lodz-landsmen*, every song sung in commemoration can qualify as a Holocaust song. As Geertz observes: "When texts lose their meaning, performances rewrite them; anyway they try to" (1986:379). In the case of the Holocaust commemoration ceremony, the texts no longer have the meaning attributed to them by their originators. Through the role of song performance in the ceremonies, the songs sacrifice their original meaning to gain instead a general, more universal significance.

A single model for conducting a commemoration ceremony has not yet been found. As long as the survivors are among us, their need to gather together will continue to determine and structure the ritual. An inevitable question arises: What will become of the ceremony after the survivors' generation has passed?

Jewish culture (as Roskies demonstrates) has a built-in mechanism for responding to large-scale calamities. That mechanism is best demonstrated in the yearly reenactment of the Exodus from Egypt, the Passover ritual. With this ritual an event of cataclysmic proportions has become formalized, and a text, the *Haggadah*—a canonical body of story, song, biblical quotations, and paraphrase—is used by observant Jews as a "guidebook" to their collective memory.

The *Haggadah* has proved quite successful in keeping a major event in Jewish history—the Egyptian captivity and subsequent redemption from slavery—before the minds of the Jewish people for some three thousand years. I would like to propose a "Haggadah of the Holocaust," along the lines of the Passover ritual. Are not events of recent times, of living memory, as essential to the central issues of Judaism, as cautionary, ethical, and transcendent as the flight from Egypt three millennia ago?

NOTES

1. Viktor Turner (1969:78–104) defines a group of people who share particular experiences and memories as a "communitas," a term that could be

used in this case. For further discussion of the term and its application in this case, please see my forthcoming article, "Interpretation of Culture through Collecting Songs from Holocaust Survivors" (Indiana University).

2. "Holocaust Day" (Yom HaShoa) for Israeli Jews falls on the twenty-seventh day of Nisan (late April to early May on the Julian calendar). The date was chosen because it is the anniversary of the uprising and liquidation of the Warsaw ghetto. However, since the uprising took place on Passover evening (the fifteenth of Nisan) and since Passover is a week-long holiday, it was decided to observe the "new" holiday on the first day of the week following Passover. In addition to the official day, individual *landsmanshaftn* have dedicated other semiofficial dates of observance.

3. The text and its translation were taken from Birnbaum (1969 : 669).

4. The exact date(s) are not known; Dobroszycki has it as August 1944.

5. Barbara Myerhoff describes the *Kaddish* as a representation of a Jewish myth: "The Kaddish makes no reference to death. It is a statement only about continuity and perpetuity; it elevates the individual who has died to a quasi-sacred level on par with the Patriarchs and Matriarchs, mythic figures with whom he or she becomes bound, suggesting the removal from history and time, sounding the theme of renewal and transcendence, of deathlessness" (in Turner and Bruner 1986 : 271).

6. The song "Oyfn veg shteyt a boym" is in Mlotek (1972 : 164).

7. The song "Zol zayn" is in Mlotek (1972 : 186) as well as in Vinkovetzky (1987, 4 : 194–95). See also Chapter 6, note 16.

8. The story of Chaim Widawski is the subject of a novel by Jurek Becker, *Jacob the Liar* (1976).

9. The song "A brivele der mamen" is in Mlotek 1972 : 144.

10. The song "Rabeynu Tam" is in Mlotek 1972 : 170.

7

Epilogue

A yidish lidl (A Yiddish Song)
Text and music by David Beyglman

In der velt kh'bin geven,
Kimat ale fir tayln oysgeforn,
Fil gehert un fil geshen,
Nor eins geblibn iz mir in mayn zikoren—
Di farshidine nigunim vos ikh hob gehert,
Di tangos, shimi's un foxtrotn.
Zay hobn far undz kayn shum vert,
Dos zaynen nor bloyz toyte notn.
Shir-hashirim iz dos shenste
Vos farfolgt mayn yedn shrit,
Fun dervaytns bald derkenst es,
Dos iz dos lid vos zingt der yid.

Refren:
Nor a yidish lidl iz dokh zayer sheyn,
Bifrat es shpilt a fidl
Hot s'lidl toyznt khen.
Ful mit harts, ful mit neshome
Brengt es nor dem yid nekhome,
Men ken fun hern keynmol vern mid.

Nor a yidish lidl hot in zikh aza koyekh,
Bifrat es shpilt a fidl,
Haylt es a krank harts oyekh,
Say in laydn in fraydn
Mit dem lid zikh shver tsu shaydn,
Nor dem taam fun a yidish lidl filt der yid.

Kh'hob gehat fraynt on a tsol,
Geshemt hobn zay zikh mit yidishkayt.
Zay gezogt kh'hob ale mol:—
Gedenkt es veln kumen andere tsaytn,
Itst zaynen zay kliger fun undz,

Ot dos zey ikh itst ayn;
Zay iz bashert nokh gute yorn,
Nokh erets gor shtil un fayn
Zaynen zay avekgefurn,
In land fun taytlen, faygn, marantsen.
Dort lebt zikh gut der yid.
Ken nokh der arbet a hoyre tantsn
Un zingen zikh dos lid.

I've been in the world,
I've traveled all over,
I heard a lot and saw plenty,
But only one thing
Remains in my memory—
The melodies that I've heard,
The tangos, fox trots and others.
These are meaningless for us,
These are only dead notes.
Song of Songs is our most beautiful one
To accompany my steps,
I can hear it from the distance,
This is the song that the Jew sings.

Refrain:
Only a Yiddish song is so beautiful,
Especially when a fiddle plays
It is even more beautiful.
Full of soul and emotions
It brings comfort to the Jew,
It is never too much to listen to.

Only a Yiddish song has so much power,
Especially when a fiddle plays,
It soothes a sick heart,
In pain and in happiness,
You don't part from the song,
Since its taste remains with you, the Jew.

I had many friends,
They were ashamed of their Jewishness.
I told them all the time:—
Remember, different times will come.
Now they are cleverer than us,
I can see them now;
They were lucky, and after some years,
To a peaceful country
They left,
In the land of dates, figs and oranges

Where a Jew lives well.
There, he can dance the Horah after work
And sing this song.

This song (from Kaczerginsky 1948 : 42–43) comprises the meaning of singing in the ghetto. The Yiddish song is a popular "universal" song and at the same time a Jewish song. It is sung in Yiddish to evoke the ancient Song of Songs. It looks for comfort in the past and hope in the future. It is not only a Yiddish song, it is a whole world. It goes beyond the actual lyrics and music.

Holocaust songs served a wide variety of functions: general entertainment, emotional expression, escape from harsh circumstances, assisting in group integration, and lastly, commemoration. They express a range of themes conveyed through both borrowed and original melodies. The value and meaning of this repertoire intimately reflect the act of singing under perilous and oppressive circumstances. The thirty-three songs studied here in terms of the survivors and their historical background, with the twenty songs added as contextual support material, illustrate the general themes of the Lodz repertoire and elaborate on the dichotomies and ambiguities that constitute the Holocaust song.

The great majority of Lodz ghetto songs concern everyday life.[1] The theme of hunger dominates this category. As mentioned in Chapter 1, starvation in Lodz was rampant, and the situation there was considered to be the worst of all the ghettos (Dawidowicz 1975 : 210).

The contextual definition of the Holocaust song becomes an issue with regard to the youth organization repertoire and, later, with the Holocaust commemoration ceremonies. The songs in both cases do not include any of the contextual themes (though both deal indirectly with the theme of "hope"). The youth organization repertoire functioned as a mechanism of escape, as entertainment and as a means of obliterating the present.

The commemoration ceremony repertoire, on the other hand, tends to idealize the period in order to offer "transcendent" messages. Thus, songs depicting the everyday life in the ghetto as one of suffering and despair are absent. Instead, the commemorators sing songs of comfort, religious belief, and love.

Most of the tunes were not composed during the time of the ghetto but were adapted from prewar sources. The melodies were drawn from three main sources: Polish popular music, German popular music (that is, the generalized Central European popular style of the period), and Jewish or Yiddish music. Only three melodies that I know of were composed in the ghetto.

Many of the songs derive from popular tunes of international character, such as tangos or marches. The selection of melodies proves the cosmopolitan background of the singers, who drew their melodies from their various musical traditions as well as from the immediate surroundings. Multilingualism clearly plays a role with regard to the language used in these compositions (Slobin 1986: 8). Each of the subjects I interviewed was multilingual, and each considered his or her linguistic resources as a factor for creative choice (this is particularly evident in the case of Miriam Harel).

With regard to the modality of the melodies, the majority (twenty-one) are in the minor mode, nine are in a major mode, and four are in *frigish*—the "Jewish scale" with an augmented second. A clear predilection for the minor mode might be noted. However, since minor modality is characteristic of Yiddish music as a whole, its predominance in this repertoire does not necessarily have any symbolic meaning.

The isolated ghetto Jews did not need to define their ethnicity in terms of the musical material they chose to perform; they used a stock of extant popular tunes, both Jewish and non-Jewish. They retained, for example, the minor mode typical of the Jewish repertoire. They did not use musical symbols to create an "identity" as did their brethren in America, who used the symbolic augmented seconds or the *frigish* mode (cf. Slobin 1980). The entire repertoire is in the standard popular form of verse and refrain; no song departed from standard rhythms or harmonies.

The context of singing clearly influenced the content of the songs. On the street corners, fearful of the authorities on the one hand and obliged to fulfill "audience requirements" on the other, the singer provided a commentary about the ongoing tragedies of the ghetto. He sang of hunger, the corrupt administration, and the ghetto police. He expressed his audience's grief and anger through his sarcasm, cynicism, and humor. And yet, singing for the entertainment of an audience who lacked basic necessities such as food, he had to express a certain amount of hope. I would note that my use of the pronoun "his" in reference to the street musicians is predicated on the fact that no account of female singers in the Lodz ghetto has come down to me or any other researcher.

At home, the singer could comment on the events and directly express his or her anger and despair, since official censorship and unofficial "audience requirements" did not affect the intimate domestic genres. On the theater stage, however, official censorship combined with audience and artistic requirements to limit the writers' expression; nevertheless their songs accurately mirror the tragic times. In contrast, the youth organization repertoire did not reflect immediate events, but rather expressed hope for a better future. In the workplace, again, the majority of songs were topical, many referring to specific local occurrences.[2]

Contexts for singing, of course, influenced the various performance styles, as in, for example, the soloistic (and thus individualistic) manner of street songs, or in the concerted "we shall overcome" choral idiom of the Zionist youth organization repertoire. In its recent context within the Holocaust commemoration ceremony, the repertoire (what remains of it), now shorn of topical references, has become the general property of professional singers.

Musical expression has the ability and power to serve a multitude of functions. John Blacking has described this power of music to create another world or "time" for the listener: "old age, death, grief, thirst, hunger, and other afflictions of this world are seen as transitory events. There is freedom from the restrictions of actual time and complete absorption in the 'Timeless Now of the Divine Spirit,' the loss of self in Being" (1969:37).

Nearly all the survivors interviewed declared that within the walls of the ghetto, singing *was* freedom, a means of escape from bitter reality even when a song text dealt with the evil events of the day.

To phrase it in psychological terms, when one sings, one creates another world. Individuals can sing wherever they wish. Singing offers a respite from everyday life. Singers transcend events, they become the song. In the ghetto, even when people sang about reality, they channeled the pain, and thus gained relief and replenishment.

The escape aspect of the repertoire serves to point out some fundamental dichotomies that emerged in the course of my study. Clearly, the counterposed notion, text/music, constitutes a central opposition. Roskies in his seminal study of Yiddish Holocaust literature observed just such an opposition in "the special power of these songs, the hidden meanings that emerge out of the essential disparity between the melody and lyrics. For just as the melody serves to mitigate the horror by recalling shared memories of the group, the lyrics insist on the radical break, on a reality so cruel that it almost defies language itself" (1984:186).

Clearly Miriam Harel's songs, each of them contrafacts of popular Polish or Yiddish melodies, comprise an example of this type of ambiguity.

It is possible, however, to elaborate on Roskies's observations because of the multilayered depth of the ghetto songs. The street songs, for example, convey a certain conventional irony, the texts lending themselves to ambiguous interpretations, overtly "pro-Rumkowski" and yet slyly seditious.

In the theater songs, fear of the authorities emerges as a theme in contrast to their seeming nonchalant lack of concern for topical affairs. The sure knowledge that these songs for public performance would be censored by the authorities led their creators to withdraw into the self-contained microcosm of the theater.

The love-hate opposition is most evident in the ghetto "hit" song "Rumkowski Chaim," where the street singer expresses his morbid dread of authority while simultaneously evidencing a childlike wish to believe that Rumkowski is the "savior of the ghetto."

The youth organization repertoire forms a further metaphoric extreme of Roskies's "radical break." Here both music and text form an ironic counterpoint to the context, an opposition which was not then apparent. "At that time we did not understand what this singing meant to us," Arieh Tal-Shir told me, "but now I understand that we were really not there—we were escaping."

Perhaps the most suggestive opposition of all is that between slavery and freedom. In a sense each of the songs testifies to this dichotomy, the creative (or re-creative) act being the ultimate, albeit in this instance private, assertion of personal liberty.

Singing in the ghetto, as well as functioning to comment on the horror of the situation, provided an avenue for the expression and communication of emotions. In the ghetto, of course, both the performers and audience belonged to the same reference group. They spoke the same language, shared similar values, beliefs, and educational backgrounds. According to Ben-Amos, "[A]udience reaction is as much a part of creation as the active imagination of the folk artist" (1972 : 7). My research tends to reinforce this generalization; the emotional content and retrospective context of the repertoire assures continuation of the creative process forty years after the event.

What then is a Holocaust song? In my introduction I suggested an expanded definition based on content and context. Thus the term is first used in its generally understood sense as a song composed in the ghettos or camps of World War II with a text relating to this particular historical period. The second classification is supplied by historical and personal context. All the songs about a particular ghetto can be categorized as Holocaust songs—whether or not they were actually composed in the ghettos and camps. Thus, performance in context—historical setting plus the singers' attributed value and meaning, rather than lyric content—is the critical factor in defining this type of Holocaust song.

The contemporary context of Holocaust commemoration ceremonies supports the second definition based on context. The fact that a song is sung in memory of the Holocaust implies that it is, at least within this particular performance context, a Holocaust song. A Holocaust song becomes the culture which defines the community, or the "communitas" which survived of that community.

What is the meaning and value of the Holocaust song? Music and song constitute a type of artistic expression different from ordinary means of communication. Musical language elevates ordinary speech, adding a transcendent level of communication to the text. As stated by Nettl, "Music in human society has the ability to abstract values" (1983 : 159).

Clearly, the central value of music in the ghetto is its vital human expression. Within an inhuman environment, the voice that continued to sing and express itself became the cry of the inmates for recognition as human beings.

The "humanizing aspect" of song is, in fact, the essential value attributed to the repertoire by the survivors. The act of singing—which is fundamentally an act of creation—was paramount in the ghetto. As such, the act of singing was an assertion of freedom as well as of life and of community.

The ghetto song symbolized survival—life, and not death. Early in this book the survivor Miriam Harel described her psychological connection to singing: "The song was the only truth." The song, as human expression, goes beyond the musical language *per se*. For the survivors it was indeed the "only truth." The songs, and their singing, tell the story of spiritual resistance.

NOTES

1. Jessica Jacoby, studying songs mainly from the Warsaw and Vilna ghettos from published sources, also finds that the majority of the songs concern everyday life in the ghetto: "Gettoaltag zwischen Adaption und Nonkonformitat: Der Anteil dieser Lieder in den Sammlungen ist sehr hoch" (1986–87 : 118).

2. In other ghettos more lullabies and songs composed by children were sung. (See Kaczerginsky 1948.) More research is clearly needed before a comparative study of Holocaust songs from the various ghettos can be attempted. The present work may inspire such research to be made before the last survivors are no longer with us.

Glossary

JEWISH AND GHETTO TERMS

Bar-mitzvah (Hebrew)—The ceremony in which a thirteen-year-old boy becomes counted among adult Jewish males.

Beirat (German)—The Jewish Council, the *Judenrat* of the ghetto.

Bund (Yiddish)—Jewish Labor Bund, the socialist labor party influential in Poland and other East European countries until World War II. As opposed to the Zionist stance of the Jewish people who return to their homeland and speak Hebrew, the Bund supported Yiddish as a national language. (See Zionism)

El male raḥamin (Hebrew)—A prayer recited in honor of the dead.

Eretz-Yisrael (Hebrew)—Land of Israel; usually used in reference to the state of Israel before its establishment in 1948 (i.e., Palestine).

Geyle Late (Yiddish)—Literally, Yellow Patch. The yellow star the Nazis forced the Jewish inhabitants to wear on their clothing to single them out and humiliate them.

Hakhsharah (Hebrew)—Zionist youth training program with a focus on agricultural work.

Halakha (Hebrew)—Jewish law.

Hanukkah (or Chanukah) (Hebrew)—A Jewish holiday celebrating the defeat of Syrian Greeks by Maccabees, 165 B.C., and rededication of desecrated Temple in Jerusalem. Known as the Feast of Lights, falls on the twenty-fifth day of *Kislev,* December on the Gregorian calendar.

Haskalah (Hebrew)—Enlightenment; the eighteenth-century movement designed to modernize Jews and their culture.

Hassidism—A mystic religious movement rapidly spread among the Jews of Poland in the second half of the eighteenth century. The movement stressed the values of piety, spiritual exaltation, and the joy of complete surrender to God.

Kaddish (Hebrew)—Part of the daily prayer; also a memorial prayer recited daily for eleven months following the death of a loved one.

Kashrut, kosher (Hebrew)—The Jewish dietary laws.

Kheyder (or Cheder) (Hebrew)—Room; elementary Hebrew school taught by the community's rabbi, or teacher.

Kibbutz (Hebrew)—Communal agricultural settlement in Israel.
Lag baomer (Hebrew)—Thirty-third day of Omer, quasi-holiday of unknown origin, celebrated as Arbor Day.
Malekh hamoves (Hebrew, Yiddish)—Angel of Death.
Man (Hebrew)—Manna, the "bread from heaven" described in the book of Exodus.
Marysin (Polish); Marishin (Yiddish)—A forested suburb of Lodz where the Jewish graveyard was located. Also located there were the orphanages, youth organization clubs, Chaim Rumkowski's summer residence, and the boardinghouse.
Mashiaḥ (Hebrew)—Messiah.
Matzot (Hebrew, pl.)—Unleavened bread, eaten during Passover as remembrance of hasty departure from Egypt with unbaked dough.
Mezuzah (Hebrew)—Doorpost; wooden, metal, or plastic container for parchment containing Bible quotations, attached to right post of gates and doors in a Jewish household (Deut. 6:9).
Minyan (Hebrew)—A quorum of ten men required for Jewish prayer services.
Mitsvah (Hebrew)—A positive commandment; a good deed.
Prezes (Polish, German)—The official nickname for the ghetto's Chairman of the Jewish Council (Chaim Rumkowski), short for "president."
Przydziel (Polish)—Food ration coupon.
Purim (Hebrew)—A Jewish holiday celebrating the rescue of the Jews from destruction during Persian exile. Masquerades, plays, and general jollity mark the day.
Rebbe (Yiddish)—A Hassidic leader (not necessarily a Rabbi).
Ressort (German, Yiddish)—A ghetto slang word for the workplace, a factory, a workshop, a job.
Rosh Hashanah—Jewish New Year; falls during September–October.
Rosh Ḥodesh—Beginning of the month for which special prayers are recited in reminiscence of the Temple period.
Shaliaḥ (Hebrew)—Emissary. Refers to Israeli emissaries sent to Europe to take care of Jewish refugees.
Shavuot (Hebrew)—Pentecost, or the Feast of Weeks. Holiday marking the acceptance of the Torah by the Children of Israel. Falls on May–June of the Julian calendar.
Shpere (Geshperre) (German, Yiddish)—Curfew. Refers to the eight days' curfew between the fifth and the twelfth of September 1942, during which more than twenty thousand ghetto inmates, elderly people, the sick, and children, were deported to the death camps.
Shtetl (Yiddish)—A small town (in East Europe).
Simḥat Torah (Hebrew)—Festival commemorating the completion of the annual cycle of Torah reading, usually celebrated with dance and song, on the eighth day of Sukot (September–October).
Sukot (Hebrew)—Feast of the Tabernacle, of ingathering, a fall harvest festival.

Talit, Taleysim (Hebrew, Yiddish)—Fringed prayer shawls worn by adult Jewish males during prayer.

Talmud (Hebrew)—Codified oral tradition perpetuating Jewish law.

Tefilah, Tfilos (Hebrew, Yiddish)—Prayer(s).

Tefilim, Tfillin (Hebrew, Yiddish)—Phylacteries: two small black leather boxes containing passages from the Bible which are bound by leather straps to the left arm and forehead and worn during weekday morning services.

Torah (Hebrew)—The Hebrew Bible, given to the people of Israel by Moses; the Jewish guideline.

Yeke, yekes—Nickname for the German and other Central European Jews deported to the ghetto at the end of summer 1941.

Yizkor (Hebrew)—Memorial prayers for the dead recited on Jewish holidays.

Yom Kippur (Hebrew)—Day of Atonement, the holiest day in the Jewish year. A day of fasting and wholehearted reconciliation with God and man.

Yortsayt (Yiddish)—Anniversary; the annual commemoration of a death.

Zionism—Movement to re-establish the State of Israel. Always in Jewish thought and prayer; directly initiated by Theodor Herzl. As a political movement, it culminated in the establishment of the Jewish State in 1948.

Selected Bibliography

Titles in Hebrew appear in transliteration in accordance with American National Standard Romanization of Hebrew publication manual (1975) as adopted by the Library of Congress. Translations of the titles are provided in parentheses.

Titles in Yiddish appear in transliteration according to YIVO's (Institute for Jewish Research) rules as adopted by the Library of Congress. Translations of the titles appear in parentheses.

Adelson, Alan, and Robert Lapides, eds.
1989 *Lodz Ghetto: Inside a Community under Siege.* New York: Viking.

Avenary, Hanoch, and Bathja Bayer
1971 "Music." In *Encyclopaedia Judaica,* vol. 12, 554–678. Jerusalem: Keter Publications.

Bauer, Yehuda
1982 *A History of the Holocaust.* New York: Franklin Watts.

Becker, Jurek
1976 *Jakob der Lugner* (Jacob the Liar). Rostock, German Dem. Rep. Verlag. (In German.)

Ben-Amos, Dan
1972 "Toward a Definition of Folklore in Context." In *Toward New Perspectives in Folklore,* edited by Americo Paredes and Richard Bauman, 3–15. Austin: University of Texas Press.

Ben-Amos, Dan, ed.
1976 *Folklore Genres.* Austin: University of Texas Press.

Ben-Menaḥem, Arieh, and Joseph Rab, eds.
1986–89 *The Chronicle of the Lodz Ghetto, 1941–1942.* 4 vols. Jerusalem: Yad Vashem. (In Hebrew.)

Beregovski, Moshe
1982 *Old Jewish Folk Music.* Edited and translated by Mark Slobin. Philadelphia: University of Pennsylvania Press.

Beregovski, Moshe, and I. Fefer
1938 *Yidishe folkslider* (Yiddish folksongs). Kiev.

Berkovits, Eliezer
1973 *Faith after the Holocaust.* New York: Ktav Publishing House.

Binder, A. W.
1971 *Studies in Jewish Music: Collected Writings of A. W. Binder.* Edited by Irene Heskes. New York: Bloch Publishing Company.

Birnbaum, Philip, trans. and annot.
1969 *Daily Prayer Book* (Ha-Siddur Ha-Shalem). New York: Hebrew Publishing Company.

Blacking, John
1969 "The Value of Music in Human Experience." *Yearbook of the International Folk Music Council,* 33–71.
1973 *How Musical Is Man?* Seattle: University of Washington Press.

Blatter, Janet, and Sybil Milton
1981 *Art of the Holocaust.* New York: Rutledge Press.

Bloom, Solomon F.
1949 "Dictator of the Lodz Ghetto: The Strange History of Mordechai Chaim Rumkowski." In *The Commentary Reader,* 30–48. New York: Atheneum, 1966.

Blumental, Nahman, ed.
1951 *Dapim leḥeker hashoah vehamered* (Research papers on the Holocaust and the resistance). Vols. 1–2:115–97. Tel Aviv: Beit Loḥamey Hagetaot. (In Hebrew.)

Bohlman, Philip
1988 *The Study of Folk Music in the Modern World.* Bloomington: Indiana University Press.
1989 *"The Land Where Two Streams Flow": Music in the German-Jewish Community of Israel.* Urbana: University of Illinois Press.

Bor, Joseph
1978 *The Terezin Requiem.* New York: Avon Bard.

Braun, Joachim
1984 "Shostakovich's Song Cycle from Jewish Folk Poetry: Aspects of Style and Meaning." In *Russian and Soviet Music: Essays for Boris Schwarz,* edited by Malcolm Brown. Ann Arbor: UMI Research Press.

Bruner, Edward
1986 "Experience and Its Expressions." In *The Anthropology of Experience,* edited by Victor Turner and Edward Bruner, 3–32. Urbana: University of Illinois Press.

Bryks, Rachmil
1961 *Der kayser in geto* (The emperor of the ghetto). New York: CYCO (Congress for Jewish Culture). (In Yiddish.)
1969 *Di papirene kroyn* (The paper crown). New York: CYCO. (In Yiddish.)

Cahan, Yehuda Leyb

1952 *Shtudyes vegn yiddisher folksshafung* (Studies in Yiddish folklore). New York: YIVO. (In Yiddish.)

1957 *Yiddishe folkslider mit melodyes* (Yiddish folksongs with melodies). New York: YIVO. (In Yiddish.)

Clifford, James

1986 "Introduction: Partial Truths." In *Writing Culture,* edited by James Clifford and George Marcus, 1–26. Berkeley and Los Angeles: University of California Press.

Dawidowicz, Lucy

1975 *The War against the Jews, 1933–1945.* Toronto: Bantam Books.

1967 *The Golden Tradition.* Boston: Beacon Press.

1977 *The Jewish Presence.* New York: Holt, Rinehart, and Winston.

Des Pres, Terrence

1976 *The Survivor: An Anatomy of Life in the Death Camps.* Oxford: Oxford University Press.

Dobroszycki, Lucjan, ed.

1984 *The Chronicle of the Lodz Ghetto, 1941–1944.* New Haven: Yale University Press.

Dobrushin, Y., and A. Yuditski

1940 *Yidishe folsklider* (Yiddish folksongs). Moscow. (In Yiddish.)

Doneson, Judith

1987 *The Holocaust in American Film.* Philadelphia: Jewish Publication Society.

Eisenberg, Azriel

1981 *Witness to the Holocaust.* New York: Pilgrim Press.

Eliach, Yaffa

1982 *Hasidic Tales of the Holocaust.* New York: Avon Books.

Fater, Isaschar

1970 *Yiddishe musik in poyln: tsvishn bayde velt milkhomes* (Jewish music in Poland: Between the two world wars). Tel Aviv: Velt Federatsie Fun Poylishe Yidn. (In Yiddish.)

Feder, Zami, ed.

1946 *Zamlung fun katset un geto lider* (A collection of songs from the camps and ghettos). Bergen Belzen: Tsentral Yidisher Komitet in Bergen Belzen. (In Yiddish.)

Fenelon, Fania

1979 *Playing for Time.* Trans. Judith Landry. New York: Berkeley Books.

Frank, Shlomo

1958 *Togbukh fun lodzer geto* (A diary of the Lodz ghetto). Tel Aviv: Hamenorah. (In Yiddish.)

Frankl, Viktor

1963 *Man's Search for Meaning.* New York: Pocket Books.

Frenkiel, Yeḥiel
1986a "Theater and Other Artistic Activities in Lodz Ghetto, 1940–1944." *Bamah Drama Quarterly* 103:12–42. (In Hebrew.)
1986b "Theater and Other Artistic Activities in Lodz Ghetto, 1940–1944, part 2." *Bamah Drama Quarterly* 104:38–60. (In Hebrew.)

Gebirtig, Mordechai
1948 *Mayne Lider* (My songs). New York: The Workmen's Circle Educational Department, 1936. (In Yiddish.)

Geertz, Clifford
1973 *The Interpretation of Cultures.* New York: Basic Books.
1986 "Making Experiences, Authoring Selves." In *The Anthropology of Experience,* edited by Victor Turner and Edward Bruner, 373–80. Urbana: University of Illinois Press.

Gefen, Menashe
1986 *Mitaḥat laa'risa o'medet gdiya* (Under the cradle stands a kid). Tel Aviv: Sifriat Poalim. (In Hebrew.)

Gelman, Yaakov
1985 "The Transformation of the Folk Song in the Ghettos and Camps." Beit Loḥamey Hagetaot. *Pirkey e'yun* 53–79. (In Hebrew.)

Georges, Robert, and Michael Jones
1980 *People Studying People: The Human Element in Fieldwork.* Berkeley: University of California Press.

Gerson-Kiwi, Edith
1958 "Judische Musik." In *Die Musik in Geschichte und Gegenwart.* Kassel: Barenreiter. (In German.)

Gerson-Kiwi, Edith, and Shlomo Hoffman
1980 "Jewish Music." In *The New Grove.* London: Macmillan.

Gilbert, Martin
1985 *The Holocaust.* New York: Holt, Rinehart, and Winston.

Ginsburg, S. M., and P. S. Marek
1901 *Evreiskie narodnye pesni v Rossii* (Jewish folksongs in Russia). St. Petersburg. (In Russian.)

Grobman, A., and D. Landes
1983 *Genocide: Critical Issues of the Holocaust.* New York: Rossel Books.

Hamm, Charles
1979 *Yesterdays.* New York: Norton.

Harel, Miriam
1989 *A'khshav kvar mutar livkot* (Now you may cry). Tel Aviv: Peretz. (In Hebrew.)

Herschlag, Judith, and Dennis Klein
1986 *The Holocaust in Books and Films: A Selected, Annotated List.* New York: Hippocrene Books.

Hertz, Aleksander
1988 *The Jews in Polish Culture.* Trans. Evanston: Northwestern University Press.

Herzog, M., B. Kirshenblatt-Gimblett, D. Miron, and R. Wisse, eds.
1980 *The Field of Yiddish.* Fourth Collection. Philadelphia: Institute for the Study of Human Issues.

Heskes, Irene
1985 *The Resource Book of Jewish Music: A Bibliographical and Topical Guide to the Book and Journal Literature and Program Material.* Westport, Conn.: Greenwood Press.

Hilberg, Raul
1961 *The Destruction of the European Jews.* Chicago: Quadrangle Books.

Howe, Irving
1976 *World of Our Fathers.* New York: Simon and Schuster.

Idelsohn, Abraham Zvi
1932a "Musical Characteristics of East European Jewish Folk Song." *Musical Quarterly* 18:634–45.
1932b *Der Volksgesang der osteuropaischen juden,* x. (Folksongs of Eastern European Jews). Leipzig: Friedrich Hofmeister.
1967 *Jewish Music in Its Historical Development.* New York: Schocken. Reprint.

Jacoby, Jessica
1986–87 "Jiddische Ghettolieder unter der deutschen Besetzung Polens und Litauens 1939–1944: Wie nahmen sie die Lagersituation, den Uberlebenswillen und Momente des Widerstands auf." (Yiddish Ghetto Songs under the German Occupation of Poland and Lithuania, 1939–1944: How They Reflect on Confinement, the Will to Survive, and the Phenomenon of Resistance). M.A. thesis, Freie Universitat Berlin. (In German.)

Jasni, Wolf
1960–66 *Di geshikhte fun yidn in lodz: in di yorn fun der daytsher yidn-oysrotung* (The history of the Jews in Lodz in the years of the German extermination). 2 vols. Tel Aviv: Hamenorah. (In Yiddish.)

Kaczerginsky, Shmerke
1948 *Lider fun di getos un lagern* (Songs of the ghettos and concentration camps). New York: CYCO. (In Yiddish.)

Kalisch, Shoshana
1985 *Yes, We Sang: Songs of the Ghettos and Concentration Camps.* New York: Harper and Row.

Karas, Joza
1985 *Music in Terezin, 1941–1945.* New York: Beaufort Books.

Kaufman Shelemay, Kay
1986 *Music, Ritual, and Falasha History.* East Lansing: African Studies Center, Michigan State University.

Kinstler, Florabel
1986 "An Eriksonian and Evaluative Investigation of the Effects of Video Testimonials upon Jewish Survivors of the Holocaust." Ph.D. diss., International College, Los Angeles.

Kipnis, Menachem
1949 *Hundert folks-lider* (One hundred folksongs). Buenos Aires: Tsentral Farband fun Poylishe Yidn in Argentine. (In Yiddish.)

Kranitz-Sanders, Lillian
1984 *Twelve Who Survived: An Oral History of the Jews of Lodz, Poland, 1930–1954.* New York: Irvington.

Kübler-Ross, Elizabeth
1969 *On Death and Dying.* New York: Macmillan.

Kugelmass, Jack, and Jonathan Boyarin
1983 *From a Ruined Garden: The Memorial Books of Polish Jewry.* New York: Schocken.

Kulisiewicz, Alexander
1974 "Z zagadnień psychopatologii muzyki i pieśni w obozach hitlerowskich" (On the psychopathological problems of music and song in the Nazi camps). *Prezegląd Lekarski* 31 (no. 1): 39–45. (In Polish.)
1977 "Muzyka i pieśń jako współczynnik samoobrong psychicznej więźniów w obozach hitlerowskich" (Music and song as a common psychological defense mechanism of victims of the Nazi camps). *Prezegląd Lekarski* 34 (no. 1): 66–77. (In Polish.)

Kviatkovski-Pinchasik, Rivka
1971 *Toyzend mol farvos* (A thousand times why?). Tel Aviv: Letste Nayes. (In Yiddish.)

Laks, Szymon
[1948] *Music of Another World.* Trans. Chester A. Kisiel, 1989. Evanston: Northwestern University Press.

Lamm, Maurice
1969 *The Jewish Way in Death and Mourning.* New York: Jonathan David.

Lammel, Inge, and Gunter Hofmeyer, eds.
1962 *Lieder aus den faschistischen Konzentrationslagern* (Songs of the Fascist concentration camps). Leipzig: Friedrich Hofmeister.

Langer, Lawrence
1986 "The Americanization of the Holocaust on Stage and Screen." In *From Hester Street to Hollywood,* edited by Sara Blacher Cohen. Bloomington: Indiana University Press.

Lanzmann, Claude
1985 *Shoah: An Oral History of the Holocaust.* The Complete Text of the Film. New York: Pantheon Books.

Levin, Nora
1968 *The Holocaust: The Destruction of European Jewry, 1933–1945.* New York: Schocken.

Lewis, Stephen, ed.
1984 *Art out of Agony: The Holocaust Theme in Literature, Sculpture and Film.* Montreal: CBS Enterprises.

Lipstadt, Deborah
1986 *Beyond Belief.* New York: Free Press.

Luel, Steven, and Paul Marcus, eds.
1984 *Psychological Reflections on the Holocaust: Selected Essays.* New York: Holocaust Awareness Institute Center for Judaic Studies, University of Denver, and Ktav Publishing House.

Marcus, George, and Michael Fischer
1986 *Anthropology as Cultural Critique: An Experimental Moment in the Human Sciences.* Chicago: University of Chicago Press.

Merriam, Alan
1964 *The Anthropology of Music.* Evanston: Northwestern University Press.

Mlotek, Eleanor
1972 *Mir trogen a gezang!* New York: The Workmen's Circle Education Department.

Mlotek, Eleanor, and Malke Gottlieb, eds.
1983 *We Are Here: Songs of the Holocaust.* New York: Hippocrene Books and Workmen's Circle Education Department.

Mlotek, Eleanor, and Joseph Mlotek, eds.
1988 *Pearls of Yiddish Song.* New York: The Workmen's Circle Education Department.

Morris, Brian
1987 *Anthropological Studies of Religion.* Cambridge: Cambridge University Press.

Myerhoff, Barbara
1978 *Number Our Days.* New York: Simon and Schuster.
1986 "'Life Not Death in Venice': Its Second Life." In *The Anthropology of Experience,* edited by Victor Turner and Edward Bruner, 261–86. Urbana: University of Illinois Press.

Nettl, Bruno
1983 *The Study of Ethnomusicology.* Urbana: University of Illinois Press.

Nketia, Kwabena
1981 "The Juncture of the Social and the Musical: The Methodology of Cultural Analysis." *The World of Music:* 22–35.

Patai, Raphael
1977 *The Jewish Mind.* New York: Charles Scribner's Sons.
Pulaver, Moishe
1963 *Geven iz a Geto* (There was a ghetto). Tel Aviv: Peretz. (In Yiddish.)
1972 *Ararat un lodzer typn* (Ararat and Lodz characters). Tel Aviv: Peretz. (In Yiddish.)
Pups, Rute
1962 *Dos lid fun geto* (The song of the ghetto). Warsaw: Yiddish-Bukh. (In Yiddish.)
Rosenfarb, Chava
1972 *Der boym fun lebn* (The tree of life). A Trilogy. Tel Aviv: Hamenorah Farlag. (In Yiddish.)
Roskies, David G.
1984 *Against the Apocalypse.* Cambridge, Mass.: Harvard University Press.
Roskies, David G., ed.
1988 *The Literature of Destruction: Jewish Responses to Catastrophe.* Philadelphia: The Jewish Publication Society.
Rosten, Leo
1968 *The Joys of Yiddish.* New York: Pocket Books.
Roth, Cecil
1970 *A History of the Jews: From Earliest Times through the Six Day War.* New York: Bantam Books.
Roth, John, and Michael Berenbaum, eds.
1989 *Holocaust: Religious and Philosophical Implications.* New York: Paragon House.
Rothmuller, Aron Marko
1954 *The Music of the Jews.* New York: A. S. Barnes.
Rubin, Ruth
1965 *Jewish Folk Songs in Yiddish and English.* New York: Oak Publications.
1979 *Voices of a People.* Philadelphia: The Jewish Publication Society.
Sandrow, Nahma
1977 *Vagabond Stars.* New York: Harper and Row.
Shpigl, Isaiah
1949 *Un gevorn iz likht* (And there was light). Warsaw: Farlag Yidish Bukh. (In Yiddish.)
1984 *Himlen nokhn shturem* (Skies after the storm). Tel Aviv: Peretz. (In Yiddish.)
Slobin, Mark
1976 "A Survey of Early Jewish-American Sheet Music (1898–1921)." *Working Papers in Yiddish and East European Jewish Studies* (YIVO) 17.
1980 "The Evolution of a Musical Symbol in Yiddish Culture." In

Studies in Jewish Folklore, edited by Frank Talmage. Cambridge, Mass.: Association for Jewish Studies.

1982 *Tenement Songs: The Popular Music of the Jewish Immigrants.* Urbana: University of Illinois Press.

1986 "Multilingualism in Folk Music Cultures." In *Explorations in Ethnomusicology: Essays in Honor of David P. McAllester,* edited by Charlotte Frisbie, 3–10. Detroit: Detroit Monographs in Musicology No. 9.

1989 *Chosen Voices: The Story of the American Cantorate.* Urbana: University of Illinois Press.

Spector, Johanna

1947 *Ghetto und Konzentration Lager Lieder aus Lettland und Litauen* (Ghetto and camp songs of Latvia and Lithuania). Vienna: AJDC.

Steiner, George

1971 *In Bluebeard's Castle: Some Notes Towards the Redefinition of Culture.* New Haven: Yale University Press.

Szeintuch, Yeḥiel

1985 "Al matsav hameḥkar" (On the state of research). In *Yedion haigud haolami lemadaey hayahadut* (Report of the International Council for Jewish Studies) 24:9–28. (In Hebrew.)

Trunk, Yeshaya

1962 *Lodzer geto* (Lodz ghetto). New York: Yad Vashem and YIVO. (In Yiddish.)

Turkov, Yanat

1968 "Teater un kontsertn in di getos un kontsentratsie lagern" (Theater and concerts in the ghettos and concentration camps). In *Yiddishe teater in eyrope . . . poyln.* (Yiddish theater in Europe . . . Poland), 464–73. New York: Aleveltlekher Yidisher Kultur Kongres.

Turner, Victor

1969 "Liminality and Communitas." In *The Ritual Process,* 78–109. Chicago: Aldine.

Turner, Victor, and Edward Bruner

1986 *The Anthropology of Experience.* Urbana: University of Illinois Press.

Vinkovetzky, Aharon, et al., eds.

1983–87 *Anthology of Yiddish Folksongs.* Vols. 1–4. Jerusalem: Magnes Press of the Hebrew University.

Web, Marek, ed.

1988 *The Documents of the Lodz Ghetto: An Inventory of the Nachman Zonabend Collection.* New York: YIVO Institute for Jewish Research.

Weinreich, Uriel

1968 *Modern English Yiddish—Yiddish English Dictionary.* New York: YIVO, McGraw-Hill.

Werb, Bret
1987 "Rumshinsky's Greatest Hits: A Chronological Survey of Yiddish-American Popular Songs, 1910–1931." M.A. thesis, University of California at Los Angeles.
Werner, Eric
1976 *A Voice Still Heard . . . The Sacred Songs of the Ashkenazi Jews.* University Park: Pennsylvania State University Press.
Whitcomb, Ian
1973 *After the Ball.* New York: Simon and Schuster.
Wiesel, Elie
1970 *Night.* New York: Bantam Books.
Wohlberg, Max
1977–78 "The Music of the Synagogue as a Source of the Yiddish Folksong." *Musica-Judaica* 2, no. 1:21–47.
Wyman, D. S.
1984 *Abandonment of the Jews.* New York: Pantheon.
Yablokoff, Herman
1968–69 *Arum der velt mit Yiddish Teater* (Around the world with Yiddish theatre). 2 vols. New York: Shulsinger. (In Yiddish.)
Zelver-Urbach, Sara
1964 *Mibaad leḥalon beiti: zikhronot migeto Lodz* (Looking through my window: Memories of Lodz Ghetto). Jerusalem: Yad Vashem. (In Hebrew.)
Zylbercweig, Zalman
1959–67 *Leksikon fun yidishn teater* (Lexicon of Yiddish Theater). 5 vols. New York: Elisheva. (In Yiddish.)
Zyskind, Sara
1981 *Stolen Years.* Trans. Marganit Inbar. New York: Signet Books.

General Index

Index of Songs

Songs of the Lodz ghetto are marked by an asterisk. Music and lyrics for those songs appear on the pages indicated in **boldface**.

A Note on the Author

Gila Flam, a native of Haifa, Israel, received her Ph.D. in music from the University of California at Los Angeles. She is the author of several articles on Israeli popular music and Yiddish music. Dr. Flam is the director of the Ethnomusicology Department of the United States Holocaust Memorial Museum in Washington, D.C.